MW00478587

# If I Don't Pass the Bar I'll Die

ASPEN PUBLISHERS

# If I Don't Pass the Bar I'll Die

## 73 Ways to Keep Stress and Worry From Affecting Your Performance On the Bar Exam

**Rosemary La Puma, Esq.**

Wolters Kluwer
Law & Business

AUSTIN   BOSTON   CHICAGO   NEW YORK   THE NETHERLANDS

© 2008 Aspen Publishers. All Rights Reserved.
http://lawschool.aspenpublishers.com

No part of this publication may be reproduced or transmitted in any form or by any means, electronic or mechanical, including photocopy, recording, or any information storage and retrieval system, without permission in writing from the publisher. Requests for permission to make copies of any part of this publication should be mailed to:

Aspen Publishers
Attn: Permissions Department
76 Ninth Avenue, 7th Floor
New York, NY   10011-5201

To contact Customer Care, e-mail customer.care@aspenpublishers.com, call 1-800-234-1660, fax 1-800-901-9075, or mail correspondence to:

Aspen Publishers
Attn: Order Department
PO Box 990
Frederick, MD 21705

Printed in the United States of America.

1 2 3 4 5 6 7 8 9 0

ISBN 978-07355-7842-5

## About Wolters Kluwer Law & Business

Wolters Kluwer Law & Business is a leading provider of research information and workflow solutions in key specialty areas. The strengths of the individual brands of Aspen Publishers, CCH, Kluwer Law International and Loislaw are aligned within Wolters Kluwer Law & Business to provide comprehensive, in-depth solutions and expert-authored content for the legal, professional and education markets.

**CCH** was founded in 1913 and has served more than four generations of business professionals and their clients. The CCH products in the Wolters Kluwer Law & Business group are highly regarded electronic and print resources for legal, securities, antitrust and trade regulation, government contracting, banking, pension, payroll, employment and labor, and healthcare reimbursement and compliance professionals.

**Aspen Publishers** is a leading information provider for attorneys, business professionals and law students. Written by preeminent authorities, Aspen products offer analytical and practical information in a range of specialty practice areas from securities law and intellectual property to mergers and acquisitions and pension/benefits. Aspen's trusted legal education resources provide professors and students with high-quality, up-to-date and effective resources for successful instruction and study in all areas of the law.

**Kluwer Law International** supplies the global business community with comprehensive English-language international legal information. Legal practitioners, corporate counsel and business executives around the world rely on the Kluwer Law International journals, loose-leafs, books and electronic products for authoritative information in many areas of international legal practice.

**Loislaw** is a premier provider of digitized legal content to small law firm practitioners of various specializations. Loislaw provides attorneys with the ability to quickly and efficiently find the necessary legal information they need, when and where they need it, by facilitating access to primary law as well as state-specific law, records, forms and treatises.

Wolters Kluwer Law & Business, a unit of Wolters Kluwer, is headquartered in New York and Riverwoods, Illinois. Wolters Kluwer is a leading multinational publisher and information services company.

# ACKNOWLEDGMENTS

I wish to thank Dr. Lewis Engel for helping me master my stress and worry, and for supporting and advising me in helping others master theirs.

I'd also like to thank my editor, Ron Nyren, for his relevant comments and gentle criticism, my book designer, Gary Klehr, who, among other things, added a whimsical touch to the book, and the general manager of the UC Hastings Law School Bookstore, John Effinger, for publication advise and assistance.

Special thanks to Paul Crabtree, Dennis Clisham, Cynthia Traina, and many others for their consistent support and encouragement. Finally, I'd like to thank my students who inspired me to write this book.

# TABLE OF CONTENTS

# INTRODUCTION

Stress and worry are normal parts of everyday life. However, they can keep you from accomplishing your goals. During the past ten years I've been teaching students how to pass the California bar exam. I've seen many students who are otherwise capable fail the bar because stress and worry diminished their academic performance. As a result, I've developed strategies to help solve these problems. These tips were developed in a variety of ways – first, from my own experience taking the bar and mastering my own stress and worry, and second, from many years of teaching students how to pass the bar exam. In researching this book, I found that many of these strategies have been proven to reduce the effects of stress and worry on test-taking.

# HOW TO USE THIS BOOK

This book assumes that you don't have a lot of time to waste and you need quick remedies to these problems—so I dispensed with most of the discussion of test anxiety research. The book can be read straight through or in parts as needed. The first part discusses mental toughness—what it is and why the bar tests it. The second part discusses the body's role in combating stress and worry, and the third, techniques for identifying and changing thoughts that affect the amount of stress and worry you feel. The fourth part provides methods to improve test-taking skills.

This is the only book that addresses solely the psychological aspects of taking such a big test. The book provides practical suggestions for dealing with stress and worry and their relatives: distractive thoughts; procrastination; and poor habits in planning, managing time studying and test taking. It is my sincere hope that it helps you.

# 1

# The Bar Exam Tests Mental Toughness

# Chapter 1

## The Bar Exam Tests Your Ability to Think Under Pressure

?? *Quick! What's the answer...?* ??

Have you ever seen an exam question you couldn't answer? By now in your academic career, the answer is probably yes, and you react to such a situation in one of two ways. The first is to calmly extrapolate from what you know to solve the problem and move on to the next. If you do this, you have a rare gift, and you don't need this book.

Most students, however, react with thoughts of doom: "Oh my God, I don't know this. I'm going to flunk. My g.p.a. will suffer. I won't get a job. I'll become a homeless person."

"Oh, my goodness, I don't know the answer to this question! Now what do I do? Everyone else seems to know the answer. Shoot, I'm running out of time, too."

It is this dialogue that prevents you from problem-solving on the spot. It steals your mental energy, wastes precious exam minutes, and distracts you. As a result, you miss important clues that would help you come up with an answer.

After such an experience, many students try to prevent this from happening again by becoming an "Information Junkie."

### *Are you an Information Junkie?*

<u>Information Junkies</u> are the students who attempt to memorize every note they take in class, every word written in the text book, and every phrase uttered by the professor. They don't feel prepared unless they know every last bit of minutiae about Consideration before entering the Contracts final. You see them in the library frantically trying to remember every possible rule, subrule, and exception to the rule. They do this because they believe that if they know everything there is to know they will avoid having to think under the stress of the exam.

*Information Junkie*

The problem with this method is that it doesn't work if you're taking an exam designed for the specific purpose of seeing how well you think under pressure, as do law school exams and the bar exam. The other problem with this method is, as in life, you can't always know everything on an exam. Thus, this know-everything-at-all-costs method is not a good solution to the problem. A better one is to develop the ability to think under pressure.

The ability to think under pressure requires mental toughness. The reason so many intelligent, capable, diligent students fail the bar exam each year is because they lack this essential skill.

So if you are a student who, when placed in an exam environment, loses your ability to think under pressure, you need this book. This book can help you develop the necessary mental toughness to pass the bar exam.

# Chapter 2

# What Is Mental Toughness?

*Mental toughness is the ability to focus all of one's thoughts on a task.*

Thus, when you have mental toughness, you can problem-solve (i.e. think) under pressure, a skill needed not only for the bar exam, but also for trying cases, negotiating settlements, taking depositions, making deals, and many other tasks lawyers perform daily.

---

## When you have mental toughness:

☞ **You are not affected by distractions from the environment or by your own negative or irrelevant thoughts and the feelings they produce.**

☞ **You stay calm under pressure, and your whole mind is available for solving the problem in front of you.**

☞ **You are capable of mental flexibility under pressure, allowing you to evaluate the many options available for solving a problem without fear, panic, or other distracting emotions.**

---

On every bar exam, a few essays will test unfamiliar areas of law. These essays will require you to evaluate the fact pattern, make up reasonable rules to sensibly resolve the issues it poses, and write a concise and organized answer. A student with mental toughness sees this type of essay and, upon realizing she doesn't know all the law that governs it, stays focused. She thinks about what she does know and extrapolates from that to solve the problem. In short, she sees such an essay as an enjoyable challenge.

Upon encountering a Will Contracts exam, **Barbara** had the following thoughts: "Gee, I don't know anything about Will Contracts. So, what do I know about Wills and what do I know about Contracts?" She calmly went about resolving the problem and she passed. This is an example of mental toughness in action. Barbara's mental toughness allowed her access to what she knew and flexibility in applying it to solve the problem.

The student without mental toughness sees the same essay as a threat, and as a result has thoughts that diminish her mental toughness. She thinks, "I don't know this. Oh my God, what am I going to do?" She becomes caught up in these thoughts and the corresponding stress, and as a result she is unable to concentrate on the problem and apply her analytical skills to it. Compare Barbara's experience to Danielle's.

**Danielle** was as well-prepared for the bar exam as Barbara. However, upon encountering a Tort exam testing Intentional Interference with Contractual Relations, she had the following thoughts: "Oh no, I didn't study this. What am I going to do? I'm running out of time and I have to write something. I should have studied those rules. Everyone else seems to know what to write. Oh God, now I'm really running out of time."

*Danielle*

Danielle's thoughts got the better of her, and as a result she wasn't able to relax and realize that probably everyone else in that room was experiencing the same problem. She was not able to control her thoughts about what she didn't know. These thoughts raised her anxiety level, which in turn eliminated her ability to explore what she did know and reasonably solve the problem. If she was calm, she would have asked questions about the cause of action, such as, "What would constitute an intentional act of interference?" and "Does "contractual relations" mean there must be an existing contract?" She would have thought about the elements of all intentional torts and extrapolated from that knowledge to solve this problem.

### What Makes the Bar Exam a Mental Toughness Exam?

The greater the weight, importance, and difficulty of an exam, the more stress and worry it raises. The greater the level of stress and worry, the greater the amount of mental toughness is needed to pass.

The bar exam has the following specific characteristics that cause stress and worry and make it a mental toughness exam. They are as follows:

1. **Long Duration**
2. **Large Amount of Material**
3. **Time Pressure**
4. **Infrequency of the Test**
5. **Atmosphere**
6. **Location**
7. **Novelty**
8. **Real and Perceived Consequences of Passing and Failing**
9. **Complexity/Difficulty**

1. **Long Duration:**
   In California the bar exam is three days, six or more hours a day. In other states, it is one to two days.
2. **Large Amount of Material:**
   The state of California tests 12 subjects: Torts, Contracts, Property, Constitutional Law, Evidence, Criminal Law and Procedure, Civil Procedure, Remedies, Wills and Trusts, Corporations, Community Property, and Professional Responsibility. Other states test more or fewer subjects.
3. **Time Pressure:**
   In California, you are given three essays in three hours with nine to 29 issues per essay on Tuesday and Thursday mornings. The Multi-State Multiple Choice Exam consists of 200 questions at 1.8 minutes per question. In California, the two three-hour Performance Tests consist of a file, a library, and instructions to draft one to three documents using the materials in accordance with directions. The Multi-State Performance Test has the same components, only it only requires the drafting of one document in 90 minutes.
4. **Infrequency of the Test:**
   In most states, the bar exam is administered twice a year, in February and July. Some states only give it once a year.
5. **Atmosphere:**
   The bar exam is given in convention centers, auditoriums, and hotel conference rooms. There are lots of people taking it and proctors are everywhere you look: at your table, at the entrances and exits, in the bathrooms. There are security checks and fingerprints, and you aren't allowed to eat or drink in the test room.
6. **Location:**
   The bar exam is not always held where you live, and thus often requires an extended stay at a hotel.
7. **Novelty:**
   Most students have never taken a test of this magnitude with the according amount of weight before.
8. **Real and Perceived Consequences of Passing and Failing:**
   The real consequences are that you will either pass and be able to work as an attorney, or you will fail and you'll have to take it again. Your perceived consequences of failing may be family and employer disapproval, loss of job, and/or personal shame.

## 9. Complexity/Difficulty:

You are expected to demonstrate good analytical, organizational, problem-solving, and writing skills under time pressure, and, of course, thorough understanding and knowledge of the law.

The characteristics above make the bar exam a high stakes test and thus a mental toughness exam. Many of these characteristics are out of your control. However, you can control your mental toughness level by addressing and eliminating as many obstacles to mental toughness as possible.

# Chapter 3

## The Biggest Obstacle's to Mental Toughness: Unmanaged Stress and Worry

Stress and worry can affect your body, cause you to behave against your own best self-interest, and produce destructive, intrusive thoughts that interfere with your ability to think under pressure. They can also diminish self-esteem and confidence.

**Your Body**

Stress and worry can affect your body in a variety of ways. The most common symptoms are increased heart rate, shortness of breath, trembling or cold and clammy hands, shaking legs, nausea, excessive sweating, lumps in the throat, dry mouth and butterflies in the stomach.

When I took the bar exam, I was quite aware of these symptoms in myself and in the people around me. The bathrooms smelled like diarrhea and vomit, and I watched a fellow test-taker swill Mylanta from the bottle. After I started teaching, one of my students reported that the woman next to her hyperventilated, turned blue, and passed out.

Clarice is an example of the extreme effects of stress and worry on the body. Your reaction might not be as intense as Clarice's. However, if you've ever felt any of the above-listed symptoms, then stress and worry have affected your body.

---

**Clarice** reported that as soon as the test started her palms began to sweat and she "froze." She found it difficult to breathe, couldn't concentrate, and wasn't able to answer any of the questions.

---

**Your Behavior**

Stress and worry can also affect your behavior. They can lead you to approach problems rigidly and thus act against your own best self-interest.

Another effect stress and worry have on behavior is the inability to adapt to change or even to be aware that the environment or conditions around you are different.

> Often, while in the middle of writing an exam answer, **Gloria** would realize that she wasn't answering the question correctly. But instead of starting again, she would continue on, because she had "already started down the path." Gloria's stress and worry kept her from acting in her own best self-interest.

> In the middle of an essay on the bar exam, **Charles** decided he needed a cigarette. He left the designated test area, although there were huge signs everywhere warning him not to leave the area while the test was in progress. When he tried to reenter after he finished his cigarette, a proctor stopped him and informed him that he would not be allowed to complete that section of the test. Charles subsequently failed.

Another example of lack of awareness is writing answers in the wrong booklet.

> **Lori** was sitting next to a woman who hyperventilated, and witnessed her being carried out of the exam room. Lori was rattled by this experience. As a result, she wrote the answer to question one in the question two book, the answer to question two in the question three book, and the answer to question three in the question one book. She failed the bar exam. (Note, if she had realized this in the exam and told the proctor she might not have.)

Stress and worry can also lead a student to put off studying for an exam, or get defensive when receiving constructive criticism about his or her work or study habits. Stress and worry can lead a student to study only part of the material tested while ignoring the rest. Take for example, Jenny, who hated multiple choice questions.

In the past, **Jenny** had not performed well on multiple choice, and now approached practicing them with trepidation. In her first few practice sessions, she missed 50%. She was very discouraged by this, although I assured her that most students miss 50% of their practice questions until about a week before the bar exam. Shortly thereafter, Jenny stopped practicing multiple choice questions altogether. When I asked her why, she said she "couldn't bear" missing them. Jenny didn't pass the exam because of her self-destructive behavior, caused by her unmanaged stress and worry.

## Your Thoughts

Finally, stress and worry can produce destructive, intrusive thoughts that interfere with your ability to think under pressure, and diminish self-esteem and confidence. Preoccupation with failure and its consequences, and ruminations about inadequate preparation and skill, are intrusive thoughts that compete for attention with the primary task of studying for and/or taking an exam. As such, they negatively affect concentration, decision-making ability, ability to take cues from the test, reading pace, and comprehension. This is because your

*Jerold*

mind is programmed to give precedence to resolving the feelings produced by these intrusive thoughts. Thus, your effort will go to pushing these thoughts away at the expense of test preparation and answering the actual test questions.

**Jerold** performed well on practice exams. However, when it came time for him to perform in the actual exam, he often felt unsure of his approach and of what was being tested. He would second-guess himself throughout the exam and then get behind and worry about the time. Further adding to his stress was the fact that he'd often wake in the middle of the night following the exam with the resolutions to these problems and then ruminate about all the points he had missed. Jerold wasn't able to solve these problems, in the actual exam because his destructive intrusive thoughts were interfering with his ability to perform at his best.

Using the exercises in this book, Jerold learned to keep his destructive, intrusive thoughts from detrimentally affecting his performance on exams, and as a result went from failing out of law school to making the Dean's List.

## Do Stress and Worry Interfere with Your Mental Toughness?
### Take This Quiz!

1. I try hard not to think about the consequences of failing the bar exam.

2. Thinking about the consequences of failing the bar exam makes me nervous.

3. It's very important that I pass the bar exam on the first try.

4. I worry about losing my job or not getting a job if I don't pass.

5. I worry about what people will think of me if I don't pass.

6. I worry about what my family will think of me if I don't pass.

7. I will feel ashamed if I don't pass.

8. I hate Real Property (or substitute any other subject you hated in law school).

9. I worry about how I will learn all the law in time for the test.

10. I worry about how I'll remember all the law.

11. I don't feel confident about my multiple choice skills.

12. I don't feel confident about my essay skills.

13. I don't feel confident about my performance test skills.

14. I don't feel confident about finishing the test in time.

15. I feel like everyone else knows what they're doing except me.

16. During final exams, I sometimes find myself thinking of things unrelated to the actual exam.

17. During final exams, I sometimes forget what I know, and then remember it after the test is over.

18. During final exams, I sometimes read exam questions without understanding them.

19. I sometimes find that my mind goes blank in an exam.

20. I sometimes feel my heart beating very fast during final exams.

21. I worry about finals after I take them.

22. I would rather write a paper than take a final exam.

23. I would do much better on final exams if I could take them without time pressure.

24. I worry about doing well on finals even when I'm really prepared.

25. My stomach is often upset before a final exam.

If you answered eight or more of these questions "True," then stress and worry interfere with your mental toughness and thus your performance on exams.

Now that you know that unmanaged stress and worry interferes with mental toughness and thus peak performance, it's time to do something about it. You can manage stress and worry so that they have minimal effect on your body, your behavior, and your thoughts. This book will help you develop the mental toughness needed to pass the bar exam.

# Chapter 4

## Mental Toughness Requires Physical, Psychological, and Intellectual Endurance

*In order to increase your mental toughness,*
*you need to build your physical,*
*psychological, and intellectual endurance.*

### • Physical Endurance

Most bar exams require a student to sit and concentrate for six hours a day for one to three days. Preparing for this exam requires even more sitting and concentrating, for up to eight hours a day five to six days a week over a six-to-eight-week period. When you have physical endurance, you can withstand the long periods of inactivity and focus your attention with ease.

### • Psychological Endurance

An important component to mental toughness is psychological endurance. Psychological endurance is the ability to remain completely focused on the task at hand under pressure. When you have psychological endurance, any negative, destructive, and distractive thoughts that may arise won't have the power to sway you. People with psychological endurance may feel anxiety, but it doesn't overwhelm them. They stay flexible, able to roll with the unexpected in an exam and let panic thoughts pass without effect.

## • Intellectual Endurance

The final component of mental toughness is intellectual endurance. Intellectual endurance comprises four major skills: the ability to understand the questions asked on an exam, the ability to use reason and problem-solving skills to answer them, the ability to express your thoughts in a well-organized, thorough, and concisely written document, and the ability to do all of this in the time allowed.

## A Word about Change

By now you've spent approximately 20 years in school, and over that 20-year period, you developed ways to cope with stress and worry. Thus, you cannot expect these coping methods to change overnight. There is no magic cure to solving this problem. Learning to manage stress and worry effectively takes time and a variety of different techniques. In addition, I guarantee you will experience setbacks. Old patterns are hard to break.

My advice is to be patient with yourself, give yourself time, and diligently practice as many of the following techniques as possible.

# 2

# Strengthening Physical Endurance

# Chapter 5

# The Body's Key Role in Overall Endurance

*Below are strategies that help to increase physical,
psychological, and intellectual endurance
all at the same time.*

### 1. Get More Exercise

Exercise is the single most important thing you
can do to improve your overall endurance, to
lower your stress and worry levels, and to
increase mental toughness. It strengthens physical stamina. It relaxes and tires the body, allowing for deep restorative sleep. It restores energy
to the body, improves concentration, and
enhances your ability to fight off disease and

heal from injury. It reduces anxiety, lifts depression, and provides a sense
of well-being and confidence. If you're just starting an exercise program,
do so gradually. You might consider a few sessions with a personal train-
er to help you set up a balanced exercise program, or you can simply start
by walking quickly 30 minutes a day, four days a week.

### 2. Improve Sleeping Habits

Deep restorative sleep is essential to physical endurance. Deep sleep
allows you to think clearly and concentrate. It repairs the body and helps
to fight off disease. Unfortunately, most law students and bar candidates
I know are sleep-deprived. Sleep-deprived students tend to get more
colds, have higher anxiety levels, and deal less skillfully with stress and
worry than those who get enough sleep.

Many students in my own bar review report poor sleep or inability to sleep during the bar prep period. This is generally caused by anxiety about the upcoming test. Often as the bar review class continues, and they see progress in their skills and work, the anxiety decreases and sleep returns. In the meantime, here are some suggestions for better sleep.

### A. Eliminate all caffeine later than 3 P.M.
Caffeine taken late in the day can affect sleep. Caffeine includes coffee, colas, teas, some pain relievers, and chocolate. Some people tolerate lots of it and sleep fine. Others don't. If you are having trouble sleeping, try this.

### B. Stop the mind chatter
Often students complain to me about mind chatter: even when they are tired, their minds just won't stop. There are several ways to put an end to mind chatter.
    a. Stop studying one to two hours before bed.
Use that time to do something relaxing, such as watching television, listening to soothing music, taking a bath, or reading a good book or magazine.
    b. Use a progressive relaxation tape. Lie in bed and listen to the tape, concentrating on relaxing each muscle one at a time.
    c. Get up and write it down. If you can't sleep because your mind won't stop or your mind wakes you from sleep, get up and write down everything your mind is saying. Don't edit. Just write. Don't stop until it is all out of your system.

### C. Use a natural sleeping aid such as Melatonin or Valerian Root
Melatonin is a naturally occurring hormone that induces sleep. By taking a bit more of it at bedtime, you encourage your mind to be quiet and go to sleep. It doesn't affect you the next day, but if you take it too often it will stop having the desired effect.

### D. Increase your physical activity
Many students can't sleep because their bodies have been sitting all day. Physical exercise, if accomplished early enough in the day (say before 8 P.M.), tires and relaxes the body, getting it ready for sleep.

### 3. Eat Well

Good nutrition keeps your body strong, your energy high, and your intellect sharp. You are also more resistant to mood swings and emotional upset. Eating well includes the following: a varied diet with lots of fresh fruits and vegetables and whole grains; a moderate amount of fat, sugar, salt, alcohol, and caffeine; and regular meal times, three or more a day.

### 4. Keep Your Life in Balance

Treat studying for the bar like a full-time job. Then spend the rest of the time taking care of the rest of you. In addition to the items above, you also need play time; that is when you do something FUN. Fun activities totally absorb your thoughts and rejuvenate you. The break from study gives your subconscious mind time to process what you've been studying, and provides perspective on the whole bar exam preparation process. Without play, your life is out of balance. This often results in feeling deprived, lethargic, bored, depressed, and uninterested in studying.

### 5. Learn and Practice Relaxation Techniques

When you are under pressure, you store tension in your muscles. You can diminish the amount of stress you feel by purposely tensing your muscles for 10 seconds and then releasing them. The more you practice doing this, the easier it will be to relax in pressure situations. Get a progressive relaxation tape and listen to it before you go to sleep at night.

### 6. Remember to Breathe

Often when you're stressed, your breathing becomes shallow; that is, you breathe from the top of your chest instead of your abdomen. Shallow breathing is uncomfortable because you don't feel as if you're getting enough air. This leads to breathing faster, which can cause hyperventilation and panic. When you hyperventilate, you don't get enough oxygen, and as a consequence you become dizzy and disoriented. If this continues for long, you lose consciousness.

So here's what you do. When you notice you're feeling stressed, check your breathing. Concentrate on relaxing the abdominal muscles. Purposely slow your movement and thoughts down. Consciously take slow, deep breaths from your abdomen. This will reduce your stress and keep you from passing out. This is a wonderful exercise because it provides a great deal of relief in a short period of time.

### 7. Meditate
Meditation is an excellent way to reduce stress and worry, increase concentration, and decrease distractibility. Meditation helps you learn to concentrate completely on the task in front of you, and to free yourself of distracting thoughts and feelings.

It takes practice, but the more you do it the easier it will become, and the less you will be bothered by annoying anxious thoughts that seem to appear in exam situations.

The easiest type of meditation I know is Zen meditation. Sit on the floor and face a blank wall. If you need back support, you can sit up against the back of a couch or the side of your bed, or you can sit in a straight-backed chair with your feet firmly on the ground. Meditation is not about being physically uncomfortable, so adjust your position until you feel good.

Next, stare at the wall and concentrate on your breath. I like to focus on the in-and-out motion of my abdomen as I breathe. Others focus on the air as it leaves the nose. (If you would prefer to do this with your eyes closed, that's okay too.)

For the next 20 minutes, watch your breath. Notice when your mind runs off and starts thinking about yesterday's ballgame, the fight you had with your coworker, or the need to find someone to stay with your cat when you go to Hawaii after the bar exam. Once you've noticed your mind has drifted away, gently bring it back to your breath. Repeat as necessary, without criticizing yourself about how many times you had to bring your focus back to your breath.

It is not important how long you stay focused on your breath. It is important that you try to stay focused and that you bring your focus back whenever you stray. It is the practice that counts even when you think it went badly.

Try to do this once a day, either first thing in the morning or last thing at night. Or find some other time, such as your lunch break. If you can't meditate for 20 minutes, start with 10 and work toward 20. Over time, you will find that meditating will make it easier to focus on studying and ignore the distracting thoughts.

# Strengthening
# Psychological Endurance

# Chapter 6

# Identifying Your Thoughts

As stated in Chapter 4, psychological endurance is the ability to focus on the task at hand, under pressure, without being affected by negative, destructive, or distracting thoughts. In addition, psychological endurance includes the ability to adjust to your environment and roll with the unexpected both during your study period and in an exam.

Thus, there are two components to it: internal and external. The internal component is the ability to concentrate completely on the task at hand and ignore unrelated thoughts. The external component is the ability to react with flexibility and problem-solve under pressure when faced with the unexpected.

This chapter and the next discuss strategies to deal with the internal component of psychological endurance: your thoughts. Chapter 8 discusses strategies for relating to your environment while under pressure. The two components are related. The more you work on the internal component, the more flexible you will be in relating to your test environment, and the better problem-solver you will become.

When you think anxious thoughts, your body reacts with the physical symptoms of stress discussed above. You can minimize these physical symptoms by changing your thoughts and your response to your thoughts. In order for this change to occur, though, you must first identify your thoughts.

## 8. The Angst Sheet

Every time you sit down to study or take a practice exam, read for class, or outline, take a piece of paper, write "Angst Sheet" at the top and place it in the corner of your desk space. While you are reading, writing, or outlining, note when your attention has wandered and you have stopped working. What are your thoughts? For five or ten minutes, just write everything that you're thinking on the Angst Sheet, without stopping your pen. Then return to your task. If you find your mind wanders again, write your thoughts down again.

On the following page is my sample angst page.

*Angst, personified*

# Angst Sheet

I can't seem to concentrate. I keep reading this property fact pattern over and over and nothing is going in.
I don't know what I'm doing.

What am I going to do?
I HATE property!!!!
What if I don't understand it before the bar exam? Then I might not pass. I have to pass. If I don't pass I can't work as a lawyer and then I won't be able to pay back my huge student loan debt. My parents will disown me and my boss will fire me and I'll be ashamed to face my friends and my boyfriend will leave me and no one will ever love me again...

The point of this exercise is twofold. The first is to become aware of your thoughts so that you can change the destructive thoughts to constructive ones. The second is to strengthen concentration. By continually bringing your concentration back to the task at hand, you are training your brain to stay on task. After using this exercise, many students reported that for the first time in their lives they heard all the negative things they said to themselves and were appalled by them.

After you've used the Angst Sheet and rated your anxiety levels for a week (see number 12 below), sit down and read through what you wrote. You might be surprised at some of the negative and critical things you say to yourself. Mark with an X each negative, judgmental, all-or-nothing, irrational, and destructive thought.

### 9. Express Your Feelings
After using the Angst Sheet for a little while, you may find that not only are you wasting valuable time and effort pushing away negative and destructive thoughts, but you are also wasting time pushing way the feelings associated with these thoughts. If this is true, then add to your Angst Sheet all the feelings you are having as well. Many students report that after using the Angst Sheet in this way and returning to

*letting go*  the essay in front of them, they see issues and facts they had missed on the first read. This happens because the "whole" of them is now focused on the essay. The part that was fighting feelings and distracting thoughts is freed, because all those thoughts and feelings are now on the Angst Sheet. Get them out on paper. They will have less effect on your work.

### 10. Watch for ALL-or-NOTHING Thoughts
In your practice with the Angst Sheet, look for all-or-nothing thoughts. These thoughts often start with "You/I never, always, can't, have to, must-n't." Here's an example of an all-or-nothing thought from one of my Angst Sheets: "I can't do multiple-choice."

I used to believe this about multiple choice. I had good reason to; I was never very good at them in school or on the SAT or the LSAT. However, the "always" part wasn't true. I performed well on many multiple-choice tests in college. I also passed the MPRE (the Multi-State Professional Responsibility Test) on the first try. Thus, the statement wasn't completely true. But whenever I took practice questions for the MBE (Multi-State Multiple Choice Bar Exam) in preparation for the bar, and incorrectly answered 50% of them, my brain used this as evidence that I couldn't do multiple choice questions. This led to thinking, "I'm going to fail because I can't do multiple choice questions," and then, "I'm not going to get a job" and then "I'm going to be poor and jobless and then homeless, etc." These thoughts, if unchecked, can spiral out of control and turn into self-fulfilling prophecies.

## 11. Name and Draw the Voice Within

When you feel stress and worry, often there are negative, demoralizing, and critical thoughts behind these feelings that impair performance. Most students try to ignore these thoughts or push them away. However, by doing this you waste precious concentration and energy, leaving little processing ability left to answer the test questions properly. However, if you can separate yourself from your thoughts and hear them as an observer, you gain perspective on them and they have much less effect on your performance. One way to do this is the Angst Sheet above. A second way is to draw and name the voice within.

Meet **Gertrude**, my inner critical voice. She wears her hair in a tight bun on top of her head, dresses way too sensibly, and is constantly wagging her finger at me. (Her picture is on the next page.) Whenever I introduce my classes to her, they laugh, because they see how ridiculous she looks and then realize how ridiculous the things she says sound. Some students report that after drawing their own voice within and naming that voice, they feel sorry for him or her, and that the voice then has little if any effect on them.

Gertrude

## 12. Rate Your Stress and Worry Level

To reduce the effect of anxiety, you have to examine the amount of it you feel in the many stages of the exam preparation process. So, when you sit down to write an essay, jot down on your Angst Sheet your anxiety level. Use a scale from 1 to 10, with 10 being so anxious you're going to throw up or pass out, and 0 being so calm you're going to fall asleep or reach enlightenment.

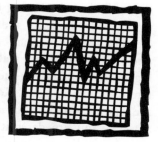

Rate your anxiety level when taking multiple-choice questions and when writing essay and performance test answers. Rate your anxiety levels before, in the middle of, and at the end of each practice. Other useful times include mornings, as you get up; night, when you go to bed; time spent in class or with friends; etc. Notice which situations are stressful and which are not. It might be you don't feel stress in the exam, but you do while you study, or vice versa. It might be that you feel anxiety only when around your peers in class.

## 13. Recognize Negative Self-Fulfilling Prophecies

A negative self-fulfilling prophecy is a prediction that comes true because you believe it and act accordingly, whether you wish to or not. You can ascertain your deepest beliefs by looking at your thoughts. If you believe you are intellectually inadequate, you will have thoughts that reflect this, such as, "I'm stupid," "I'm dumb," "So-and-so is smarter than me," "I'm no good at (fill in the blank)," "When they figure out I've been faking it they'll throw me out for sure," or "I'm not smart enough to do this."

These thoughts translate— often without your knowledge— into behavior that is incompatible with succeeding. Your thoughts distract you from the task at hand and impede your judgment. Consequently, you behave in ways contrary to your ultimate goal. The opposite is also true. If you believe you are capable of solving problems and achieving your goals, then you are more likely to behave in ways that do just that.

## 14. Tape Your Compulsive Thoughts

If you find you're having the same destructive thoughts repeatedly, try taping your thoughts and listening to them. Speak them into a tape recorder, then play them back, listening carefully. When you've finished, rate your anxiety on a scale of 1 to 10. The more anxiety you feel, the higher the number you should choose. Then listen to the tape again and rate your anxiety again. Repeat this process a few more times. Then put the tape away and do the same thing the next day. Do this every day for a week. You are desensitizing yourself to your destructive, obsessive thoughts by listening to them outside your head (objectively) as opposed to being subjected to them inside your head.

# Chapter 7

# Change Your Thoughts

Once you've identified your thoughts, you can change how you react to them, and in turn you can replace them with more objective ones. As you learn to change your reactions, stress and worry will affect you less and your mental toughness will increase. Although this sounds simple to do, in reality it takes time and practice. The key here is to be patient with yourself. Don't expect your thoughts or your reactions, which have developed over a number of years, to change overnight. Below are some strategies for changing your thoughts.

## 15. Put the Voice on Trial

To get control of the negative voice inside, make the voice produce evidence to support the truth of what it says. On a piece of paper label four columns: The Voice, Evidence to Support, Evaluation of Evidence, Voice Revised.

In the first column write the destructive or all-or-nothing thought. Then ask yourself if there is any evidence to support this thought. Write whatever evidence you have in the second column. Then evaluate this evidence in the third column and see if it is truly enough to prove the truth of the negative or all-or-nothing thought. If not, then revise the thought so it is more accurate and then evaluate its truth in the same way. Eventually, you will get to the root feeling and belief behind the voice, which usually is fear: fear of failing, fear of succeeding. Here's an example:

| THE VOICE | EVIDENCE TO SUPPORT | EVALUATION OF EVIDENCE | VOICE REVISED |
|---|---|---|---|
| God, you're an idiot. | You got C's in law school. | This doesn't mean I'm an idiot. | Okay, you won't be successful. |

→

| | | | |
|---|---|---|---|
| Okay, you won't be successful. | You got C's in law school. | C's in school don't mean I won't be successful. | Okay, you're not going to perform better in school. |

→

| | | | |
|---|---|---|---|
| Okay, you're not going to perform better in school | Straight C's in law school. | This does not mean I won't do better in school. | Okay, I am afraid I won't perform any better. |

Once you get to the fear, acknowledge it. It will pass if you let yourself feel it, and you will be more capable of acting constructively.

## 16. Persistently and Diligently Go after Your Negative, Destructive, and All-or-Nothing Thoughts

To stop negative, destructive, or all-or-nothing thoughts keeping you from performing your best on the bar exam, you have to identify, analyze, and revise your thoughts. Remember, you have been thinking this way for years, and so it will take time, patience, and diligence to change these thoughts. Whenever you notice your stress level is high or you're worrying about something, stop what you are doing and do something that moment to address it. Use the Angst Sheet to identify what you were thinking that caused your stress level to go up. Write down your worries, examine them objectively for reasonableness, and think of ways to address them. Use the breathing and relaxation techniques previously mentioned to center and calm yourself.

## 17. Have Realistic Expectations

You don't expect a baby to crawl one day and run a marathon the next. A baby needs to learn to crawl first, then walk and fall down a lot, then run, etc. Yet time and time again students expect to earn a high score on their very first practice exam. They expect to correctly answer every multiple choice they take, although they may not have studied the subject for several years. This is unrealistic. When these students inevitably perform poorly on their practice essays or miss 50% of their multiple choice questions, they can become depressed and demoralized, and feel like giving up.

The bar study period is six weeks for a reason. It takes time to bring your skills up to speed. This is especially true if you graduated from law school without a clue as to what is expected on law school exams. You should expect to make slow, steady progress. You should expect that the first draft of every essay you write will be awful, and that you will incorrectly answer 50% of multiple choice questions until one to two weeks before the bar exam.

## 18. Celebrate Your Incorrect Multiple Choice Answers and Poorly Written Essay Exams

In addition to having realistic expectations, you should also celebrate every incorrect multiple-choice question and every poorly written essay exam. When you take 20 multiple choice questions and you miss half of them, instead of assuming this is evidence of your inability, throw a celebration and say to yourself, "Great, that's 10 more I'll get correct on the exam." Then analyze each one methodically to find out why you missed it. (More about how to do this in Chapter 9.)

## 19. Deal with Your Doubt

I once had a student who, after answering a question, would then second-guess her decision. She could not rid herself of this doubt until she had checked and rechecked her answers. Then, while rechecking her answers, she'd get confused about what she knew and didn't know. As a result, she would change many of her correct answers to incorrect ones.

Doubt is fine when there is a good reason supporting it. When it is just undermining you for no real reason, it will hurt you. Your job is to figure out when doubt is substantiated by solid evidence and when it is not. When you feel doubt, write it on a separate piece of paper and evaluate it objectively. See if there is any valid reason, based in fact or law or logic, for why your doubt might be right. If not, ignore it.

## 20. Don't Let a Silly Test Determine Your Self-Worth

Have you ever received a bad grade, and instead of thinking, "I'm stupid, I'm dumb, I can't do anything, I'm an idiot," you thought, "I guess I didn't do well on that test at that moment in time. I'll have to take a look at it and see what happened." Probably not. This is because you were raised from a young age to believe that if you got a good grade you were a good, smart little boy or girl, and if you got a bad grade you were bad and dumb. Thus, you grew up having your self-worth yanked about every time you received a grade on a test. Some students who never learned to test well believe that they are dumb, without realizing that they never learned to test well.

Who decided that if you did well on tests, you were smart and good, and if you did poorly, you were dumb and bad? Schools did. It is a way to process thousands of students through a school system. It is easier to dismiss a student who didn't do well on a test than teach to each one's individual needs and skills. It's cost efficient. Otherwise how would we determine who gets to go to Stanford Law School and who doesn't? How would we determine who works at Pillsbury, Madison and Sutro (a prominent San Francisco-based law firm) and who doesn't? Standardized tests mean little or nothing about anything important. They just indicate who naturally tests well (or learned to somewhere along the way) and who doesn't. Most people can learn to test well.

If you are studying for the bar exam and you feel stress and worry, it is very possible that your self-worth is connected to passing it. This connection will make it much harder to pass the exam, and more likely that you will fail and end up in a self-destructive tail spin.

I can personally vouch for what happens when you attach your self-worth to passing the bar exam. After I failed the bar I went into a severe depression. I had little appetite and I was barely capable of going to work each day. I had a rather severe, but not uncommon, reaction. After reflecting on why, I realized that as a child my siblings and I were only valued if we got A's and B's, and we were punished severely if we got anything else. Additionally, my father didn't want me to go to law school and told me I would fail if I went. These two experiences greatly affected my ability to perform under pressure and believe in myself. Thus when I failed, I believed I was worthless.

The point is that you need to find your worth outside of the bar exam. After all, the bar exam is just a test.

### 21. Deal with Feeling "It's Not Fair"

**Alvan** was a bright student. He knew the law and understood how to apply it. He was great in class, but in the exam he would go straight to the heart of the problem, missing all the little steps of logic leading up to his conclusion. Thus, Alvan consistently got C's. When I quizzed him about this, he said it seemed like such a waste of time to have to do all the foundational work. He didn't want to be bothered with it, yet he still wanted a good grade. So I

*Alvan*

said to him, "So you just can't be bothered with showing the grader all your thoughts, all the steps that led to your conclusion, even though that is exactly what the grader wants." "Yes," he replied. "Why?" I asked. He thought for awhile and said, "I shouldn't have to."

Alvan was expressing a powerful destructive belief: "It's not fair." Once he realized this belief was behind his behavior, he was able to begin the process of accepting it. Once he did that, he gained control over his impulse to go straight to the conclusion, and learned to lay out methodically his analysis.

### 22. Avoid Comparing Yourself to Others

At least once a semester a student will tell me that everyone else is doing better than she is. When a student says this, the first thing I ask her is how she knows that everyone else is doing better than she? The response is usually mumbled because the truth is that she has no way of knowing. Sometimes a student will substantiate her belief that everyone else is performing better than she by saying that some other student never studies and gets A's. My response is this: "How do you know he never studies? Are you with him 24 hours a day?"

There are two things you should remember when you start comparing yourself to other students. The first is that your peers lie. The second is, even if what they say or do is true, so what?

Students in law school by nature are generally highly driven, ambitious and competitive. Most of them did well in college and thus are shocked and ashamed when they don't do as well in law school. Law school student bodies consist of students who were in the top 10-20% of their class in college and are accustomed to receiving A's. Thus, when these same students get C's in law school they usually feel shame, and to hide that shame they lie. They lie about grades, study habits, and job opportunities just to save face and on occasion to put doubt in you, the listener, in your own achievement. Remember this when someone boasts about never studying. It is simply not true.

Occasionally, however, it may appear to be true. There is often one student in a law school class who is able to process and analyze all the concepts learned in law school in his head. Thus, it appears on the outside that he is not studying, i.e. taking notes, writing outlines and taking practice exams. This isn't true. He is doing all these things, only he is just capable of doing all of it in his head. It doesn't make him better or worse than you.

This leads me to the second thing to remember when comparing yourself to others. So what? So what, if he or she can do all this in his or her head? Often this type of student has no personal skills and is lousy in bed. You know the student at the top of the class who is so odd that no one wants to hang out with him or her? He or she probably won't get a job because a big part of what an employer looks for besides competence is, would he or she like to have lunch with this person everyday. If the answer is no, you're not going to get the job no matter what you are capable of doing in your head.

So don't compare yourself to others. First, you don't know what others do to prepare because you can't be with them 24 hours a day. Second, you have strengths and weaknesses that are all your own. So does the person you're comparing yourself to. He or she has weaknesses that you don't see and you wouldn't want. Comparing yourself to others is a trap from which you can never escape. When you compare yourself to others, either you are better or worse than others, which makes you conceited and a snob, or you have no self-esteem or self-worth. See people as they are. They have some skills that you don't have and some deficits that you don't have. These don't make them better or worse than you.

### 23. Ask "So What?" to "What If?" Thoughts
"What if" starts many worry thoughts. "What if I don't pass the bar?"

"What if I don't get an A?" "What if I don't have a great g.p.a.?" "What if I don't get a job?" "What if I can't pay off my student loans?"

An onslaught of ominous prophecies that are often not true often follow "What if" thoughts. When you think "What if" you give the worry wart inside of you permission to give you something to worry about and in turn it will give you the worst scenarios to worry about. Here's an example:
You: *What if I don't pass the bar?*
Your head: *Oh my God, I can't even think about the possibility. My life will fall apart. I'll have no money and no way to make money because I can't practice without a license. I'll lose the job I've been offered. I won't be able to pay my rent, my bills, or my huge student loan payment and I'll have to take the bar exam again.*

Often this tirade can expand into unrelated areas as well. "I'm going to lose my wife, girlfriend, boyfriend, lover, significant other, husband" or "My parents will disown me" or "I'm going to be out on the street with no home and no money," are all good examples of this expansion. The result of all these thoughts is stress, pressure and worry which can certainly make you fail. Instead ask yourself "So What?"

**You:** *What if I don't pass the bar exam?*

**Your response:** *So what if I don't pass?*

**You:** *I'll lose my job.*

**Your response:** *Yes I will. So what?*

**You:** *I'll be upset and disappointed and I will have financial problems.*

**Your response:** *So what?*

**You:** *I will have to take the bar exam again and I won't have any money.*

**Your response:** *So what?*

**You:** *How will I manage?*

**Your response:** *You'll figure it out.*

The whole point of the exercise is to show you that you won't die and your life won't fall apart. Yes, you will be disappointed if you lose a job, and yes, you may not have any money, and yes you'll be upset that you have to take the bar again, but it isn't the end of the world which is what your mind would have you believe it is. As long as you believe the voice that says your life will fall apart if you don't pass, you will create enormous pressure and stress for yourself that will make failing a greater possibility than without it.

## 24. Examine and Accept the Worst Case Scenario
If you can face the worst case scenario, losing your job, not having any money, having to take the bar exam again, and be okay with it, you'll lift a huge amount of pressure, stress and worry from your shoulders. Once that is lifted, academic improvement is inevitable.

There are two types of students in my bar review: Those that have faced the worst case scenario and are okay with it and those who haven't. Those that have, improve and as a result their confidence rises too. Those who haven't, improve very slowly which makes the pressure and stress from the "What if I don't pass?" thought even bigger. It's an endless circle, either an upward one in the former or a downward one in the latter. You can either not examine the worst case scenario (and wind up a huge bundle of nerves that will precipitate failing) or make peace with it and increase your chances of passing.

There is a saying about love that applies here. The saying is that if you love something let it go and it will come back to you. The same is true for the bar exam. The more tightly you hold on to needing to pass it, the more likely you are to fail it.

## 25. Avoid Blaming Others for Your Troubles
Often students will tell me the reason they failed the bar is because their boss wouldn't give them time off, their boyfriend or girlfriend picked a fight with them the day before, or they had to work, or they got married or someone in their family died or got sick or got married, or they had a bad professor for contracts. These are all examples of blaming others for your troubles. If you failed the bar exam it is because of what you did or didn't do before or during the exam.

One student told me that she didn't pass because she had to work for the three days before the bar exam. She further explained that if she had had those days to study she would have passed. This is nonsense. Firstly, she sabotaged her performance by putting her job above her bar preparation. Secondly, the bar exam requires preparation over a long period of time, 6-

8 weeks, plus three years in law school. Three days one way or another won't make a difference between passing and not if the person was properly prepared in the first place.

Take responsibility. If your priorities, are wrong make them right.

## 26. Avoid Punishing Yourself
The learning process in college is quite different from the learning process in law school. The latter requires that you make mistakes and learn from those mistakes. In the former, you just memorize all the material and regurgitate it on the exam. Law school and bar exams require that you explain the law and how it works with different fact patterns, in language a layperson would understand. The most efficient and effective way to learn to do this is to write practice exams on different hypothetical situations and then examine the sample answers, figure out where you went wrong, and write them again. This means you have to be okay with making mistakes.

In my experience, many law students and bar applicants are not okay with making mistakes. Many of them punish themselves for every issue missed, incorrect law applied, and disorganized answer written. These students mistakenly believe that self-punishment is a good way to motivate themselves to improve. However, in my experience, the less a student engages in self-punishment, the faster he or she acquires the skills needed to pass the bar exam. In addition, these students are often more motivated to continue their work than those who engage in self-punishment, because they don't feel demoralized.

The learning process for passing the bar exam requires that you make mistakes to improve your knowledge and skills. Thus, punishing yourself for these mistakes wastes energy, destroys morale and self-esteem, and interferes with acquisition of skills.

## 27. Remind Yourself How Far You've Come
If you are like most law students and bar applicants, you have never received a grade lower than a B before, let alone failed a test like the bar exam. Thus, it is a shock when you get your first C (or B when you've never received less than A's) or when you fail the bar exam. Under this shock, students often view this one incident as a measure of their intelli-

gence, which clearly it is not. This is a good time to remind yourself that you can't lose your intelligence overnight, that C's in law school or failing the bar exam is not evidence that the last 25 or so years you were really stupid. It just means you haven't figured out the game yet.

## 28. Treat Yourself Like You Would Your Own Six-Year-Old Child

If you are punishing yourself for performing poorly, try to treat yourself like you would your own six-year-old child. Ask yourself this: If you had  a six-year-old child who you knew had studied for his spelling test, yet he still failed, would you say to him all the things you're saying to yourself? If the answer is no, then ask yourself, why am I saying these things to myself? You'd probably say to the child, "Well I know you put in the time to prepare, so let's figure out what went wrong and try again." Try saying this to yourself instead. All the other stuff, the punishing and the blaming and the berating, just gets in the way of learning and progress.

## 29. Consider the Positive Words of Others

At some time in your academic career, someone said something positive to you about your ability. Think about when you last experienced thoughtful praise from a respected peer or professor. This is the time to remember it. It will give you confidence to continue when you don't feel like it.

# Chapter 8

# Relating to Your Environment

The following strategies will help you relate to your environment while under pressure, during both the study period and the exam itself.

### 30. Get Support
When you're going through a stressful event like preparing for the bar exam, you need supportive friends and family. Anyone who is not supportive you should remove from your support system. Unsupportive people are those who are critical, judgmental, or mean, or who don't want you to succeed, don't believe you can succeed, or think that haranguing you helps. Sometimes friends and family, either consciously or unconsciously, can be this way. If so, find others who will be there for you and encourage you when you're down.

### 31. Diminish Exposure to Naysayers
If you hang around naysayers and negative, hopeless, cynical people, they will bring you down with them. So ditch them.

### 32. Set the Ground Rules with Your Family and Friends
Before beginning your preparation for the bar exam, you need to first lay down some ground rules with your family and friends and loved ones.

You can't control life. It will continue to happen. People will die, get cancer, have accidents, etc. However, you can explain to those around you what the six-to-eight week marathon that precedes the test is all about, and describe its importance to your career and life. Sit down with your family, friends, wife, husband, significant other, lover, and/or boss and tell them you are not available for the next six to eight weeks. Ask them to not fight with you, leave you, fire you, or argue with you during this time. Tell them you need to be completely selfish for the next six to eight weeks, and that you cannot be required to go to family events, church, work, or anything else. Tell them you will be unavailable to take care of the kids, mow the lawn, cook, clean, or do any other chores or responsibilities. Ask them to respect your wishes in this area, because if they do, the whole process will go more smoothly and you might not have to repeat the exam.

This speech won't guarantee that your family, responsibilities, and job won't interfere, but if they truly care about you, they will think twice about disturbing you.

### 33. Make Reasonable Decisions Based on the Facts
On occasion, events will occur that are beyond your control. Just because you're taking the bar doesn't mean life stops. People die, get cancer, get divorced, lose their jobs, etc. The big test is how you deal with these events when they intersect with your bar preparation.

I've had many students who found out, right before or in the middle of the bar preparation period, that their parent had cancer, or their sibling needed a kidney transplant, or their parent or loved one was dying. I advised them to take some time off to deal with the loss and take the bar exam the next time. They needed time to deal with issues that are infinitely more important than the bar exam. When students don't take my advice, they become so distracted by worry and grief that they inevitably fail the test and have to take it again anyway.

Often students do not want to follow this advice because it means waiting another six months to take the test and another year to start their careers. To them I say, life is long. Six months or a year out of your life is nothing. You have the rest of your life to work, but when death is nearby you have little time.

Here's an example of some good decision making. **Dean** was about to begin studying for the bar exam when his brother got word that he was to have a kidney transplant immediately. I advised Dean to postpone his preparation for the bar exam to be with his brother during the surgery and recuperation. He assured me he wasn't worried about his brother and that he could do both. However, two weeks into my bar course, he came to me and said he needed to be with his brother, and thus was postponing his preparation for the bar exam. Six months later he prepared and sat for the bar exam and passed. Dean made a reasonable decision based on the facts as he obtained them. He wasn't rigid about his decision to take the bar exam, and this flexibility prevented him from failing another time.

Ultimately, you have to be the judge of when you should take the exam and when you should wait. Keep the bar exam in perspective. It is, after all, just a test. Be clear about your priorities, because if you're not, the distraction will keep you from passing the bar.

## 34. Acknowledge How Little Control You Have Over Life

This is related to number 33 above. Unfortunately, life doesn't always cooperate when you're training for an event like the bar exam. People die, get cancer, move away, file for divorce, and lose their jobs. It is helpful when you are in such a situation to acknowledge this: YOU ARE NOT IN CONTROL. You can't control the weather or disease or death or what other people do.

However, you can control your response to these events, as long as you don't ignore their existence. Acknowledge them and give yourself adequate time and space to process them. If you ignore them, they will impede your progress and interfere with your performance.

Here are some examples of good problem-solving. I had a student, **Jerry,** who was diagnosed with a cancer a week before final exams. He needed to have surgery immediately. Instead of trying to take finals at their scheduled time, have surgery, and deal with the emotional fallout of cancer, he postponed his finals until he recovered from surgery.

Another student, **Mary,** was trying to study for the bar exam while her mother was being treated for breast cancer. Because of this, Mary was distracted in class and couldn't concentrate. Mary had several options. She could sit the bar out one season and take it when her mother was better, or she could attend to her feelings and thoughts about her mother's health so that she could focus in class. She chose the latter and started therapy. Within two weeks, her concentration increased and she passed the bar.

Mary passed because she didn't attempt to repress all her feelings about her mother's health while preparing for the bar exam, something I've seen a number of students attempt without success. When Mary tried to repress her feelings, she became distracted and couldn't concentrate. However, when she faced them directly in therapy, their effect on her performance diminished and she was able to take the bar without further interference from them.

Mary acknowledged that she didn't have control over her mother's health, but did have control over her response to the situation. She faced her thoughts and feelings, got information about her mother's condition, and made realistic decisions surrounding this life event. Consequently, her performance on the bar was less affected by it and she passed.

### 35. Be Flexible
In the example above, Mary decided to deal with her worry about her mother's cancer in therapy and continue her studies for the bar. However, she remained flexible. She was prepared to walk away from her studying if her mother's condition worsened. We saw this flexibility in Dean's behavior as well. (See number 33.) He thought he could handle his brother's kidney transplant and take the bar exam, but as the days progressed he realized he would be distracted by it, and so postponed his bar preparation.

Flexibility in thinking and planning is necessary to passing the bar exam. A big part of what the bar examiners are testing is your ability to solve problems under pressure.

I guarantee that the exam will test issues that you didn't study or don't know. The examiners include unfamiliar material purposely, because as a lawyer, you won't always know the law. The examiners want to see how well you problem-solve under pressure. To do this, you must be flexible under pressure. If you're rigid, it is almost impossible to think of different options and evaluate them objectively for their effectiveness. Rigidity also leads to narrow thinking.

So remember, flexibility in your decisions and planning is key. Facts change, situations change. You have to be ready to adjust, both in your studying for the bar, and in the exam itself.

## 36. Desensitize Yourself

One of the best ways to reduce feelings of pressure when taking an exam is to desensitize yourself to the experience. You can do this by taking exams often.

Students take over 100 exams in my bar tutorial. Each week, they take four exams in class and 8 to10 exams outside of class on one to two subjects. They do this every week for the six-to-eight-week period before the bar exam. At the beginning of the study period, students are nervous when I administer each day's practice exam. However, by the end of the study period, the tension is half of what it was on the first day of class.

After the bar exam, my students often report that they felt less stress and pressure while taking the bar exam than they did taking finals in law school. They also report that they were more flexible during the test and were able to adjust to the circumstances around them more than when they took law school exams.

The reason? In addition to learning good test-taking skills, these students became desensitized to the test environment by repeated exposure. Consequently, they didn't feel large amounts of pressure and stress while taking the exam and were more able to remain flexible. This in turn allowed them to problem-solve effectively under the pressure of the exam.

So if taking tests makes you feel stressed, get over it by taking them everyday. I often suggest that my students form groups of two to four people and agree to meet in the library every day at 6 P.M. to take a test. If you know others will be coming, it makes it easier to do it.

## 37. Use Visualization to Reduce Stress

If the thought of going into an exam room causes stress, then the actual event will be much worse. To minimize this anxiety, sit down in a quiet place, close your eyes, and visualize the exam room in as much detail as you can. Next, visualize walking into it and sitting down. Visualize the other people in the room, the proctors, other students. Visualize the test starting and you taking it. Now stop and rate your anxiety level. Do this every day for a week. Again, the principle of this is the same as in numbers 35 and 36 above. You're desensitizing yourself to stressful situations. This doesn't mean you won't feel any stress in the real situation. But you will feel less stress, and as a result, will be more able to perform under pressure.

You can also use visualization in the test itself or any time you need to reduce your stress. Think of a place where you feel calm and at peace, and visualize it in detail. Or, if your confidence in your ability is low, visualize an activity you're good at. A number of my students have used these two specific visualizations successfully to keep themselves focused on the exam itself when they began to be distracted by feelings of stress or worry.

# Strengthening Intellectual Endurance

# Chapter 9

# Plan Your Study Period

Intellectual Endurance consists of five major skills: responsiveness, reasoning, problem-solving, concise writing and time management. You will notice that memorization is not one of them. This is because you need a basic <u>understanding</u> of the law to pass the bar exam. Rote memoriza-  tion will not give you this understanding. The bar exam tests <u>skills</u>. The examiners want to see the skills above used in conjunction with your basic knowledge of the law.

This chapter and chapters 10 through 12 will help you develop the five major skills that comprise Intellectual Endurance. Below are tips on planning and using your time efficiently and effectively, and ways to improve your essay, multiple-choice, and performance test skills. Also included are three self-grading questionnaires, one each for grading essays, multiple-choice questions, and performance tests. These questionnaires include all the questions I ask when I am grading a student's exam. I drafted them after a frustrating day of teaching and have used them with great success ever since. I urge you to use them and all the other tips in this chapter to improve your Intellectual Endurance.

## 38. Calendar Your Life

In order to accomplish the many tasks needed to prepare for and successfully pass the bar exam, you have to plan. An extra benefit of this planning is that it will also reduce your stress level. If you know what you're going to do every day, and know that you have time built in to do everything, your anxiety will stay low and you'll accomplish more. Here are some guidelines for how to "calendar" your life.

First determine the number of subjects you need to review. California, where I teach, tests in 14 subjects. They are Torts, Contracts, Real Property, Constitutional Law, Evidence, Criminal Law, Criminal Procedure, Civil Procedure, Wills, Trusts, Corporations, Community Property, Remedies, and Professional Responsibility. I pare them down to 12 by adding Remedies to the end of my Torts, Contracts, and Real Property outlines and by pairing Criminal Law with Criminal Procedure and Wills with Trusts. The first six are referred to as the MBE subjects because they are tested on the Multistate Bar Exam (MBE), a 200-question multiple-choice exam given on the second day of the California Bar Exam.

After you determine the number of subjects you need to study, get a big blank calendar for the months of May, June, and July. (I will be using these months as an example because all states give the exam in July. Of course, if you are in a state that offers the exam in February as well, the same planning applies. Just substitute December for May, January for June, and February for July.) Start by marking off the bar exam days. The bar exam for every state that uses the Multistate Bar Exam multiple-choice questions will always include the last Wednesday in July (February).

Here's an example:

| SUN | MON | TUE | WED | THURS | FRI | SAT |
|-----|-----|-----|-----|-------|-----|-----|
| July 28 | 29 | 30<br>Bar Exam | 31<br>Bar Exam | Aug 1<br>Bar Exam | 2 | 3 |

While you're crossing off the bar exam days, cross off the day before and label it OFF. Then mark the seven days before that day for memorization of your approach outlines. (We'll discuss what these are later.)

| SUN | MON | TUE | WED | THURS | FRI | SAT |
|---|---|---|---|---|---|---|
| July 21 Memorize | 22 Memorize | 23 Memorize | 24 Memorize | 25 Memorize | 26 Memorize | 27 Memorize |
| 28 | 29 OFF | 30 Bar Exam | 31 Bar Exam | Aug 1 Bar Exam | 2 | 3 |

From this point, schedule in your subjects. Schedule in all your non-MBE subjects. In California, they are Civil Procedure, Community Property, Corporations, Professional Responsibility, Remedies, and Wills and Trusts. These subjects don't have as much to them as the MBE subjects, so allot your days accordingly. Here are some guidelines: Civil Procedure—4 days, Wills and Trusts—four days, Corporations—3 days, Community Property—three days, Professional Responsibility—2 days. Instead of studying Remedies separately, I simply put the tort remedies with my tort study period, the contract remedies with my contract study period, and the property remedies with my property study period.

Next, schedule your study of the MBE subjects for June. You should be completely done with them by the end of the month. Here are some guidelines: Torts, Contracts, Real Property—four days, Evidence—three days, Criminal Law and Procedure—four days.

Next, plan time to take performance exams. I like students to practice these exams in the afternoon, since that is when they are given. Plan to take an exam each Saturday afternoon in June from 1 P.M. to 4 P.M. After allowing for a short break, review the answer and rewrite as needed from 6 to 8 P.M., or the morning of the next day. Next, label Saturday mornings "Makeup Time." Use this time to make up work that you didn't complete during the week. Don't schedule anything for Sunday. Take Sundays off unless you get really behind.

Finally, schedule at least one simulated exam. In my bar review course, I give several simulated exams including a half-bar-exam. The latter consists of three essays in the morning of the first day, one performance test that same afternoon, and 100 multiple-choice questions on the morning of the next day. I'm not a believer in taking a full bar exam so close to the real one. You need to peak at the right time. It is common knowledge that if you can run three miles you can run a 10K race (approximately seven miles). I believe the same applies here: if you can do half a bar exam, you can do a whole one. Use the second half of the second day to review and rewrite if necessary your essays, performance test and multiple-choice questions.

Here's an example of what your calendar should look like so far:

| SUN | MON | TUES | WED | THURS | FRI | SAT |
|---|---|---|---|---|---|---|
| June 2 | 3<br>Torts<br>Rems | 4<br>Torts<br>Rems | 5<br>Torts<br>Rems | 6<br>Contracts<br>Rems | 7<br>Contracts<br>Rems | 8<br>Makeup Time<br>9-11 am<br>Performance<br>Test 1-4 pm |
| 9 | 10<br>Contracts<br>Rems | 11<br>Contracts<br>Rems | 12<br>Property<br>Rems | 13<br>Property<br>Rems | 14<br>Property<br>Rems | 15<br>Makeup Time<br>9-11 am<br>Performance<br>Test 1-4 pm |
| 16 | 17<br>Con Law | 18<br>Con Law | 19<br>Con Law | 20<br>Evidence | 21<br>Evidence | 22<br>Makeup Time<br>9-11 am<br>Performance<br>Test 1-4 pm |
| 23 | 24<br>Evidence | 25<br>Criminal Law<br>& Procedure | 26<br>Criminal Law<br>& Procedure | 27<br>Criminal Law<br>& Procedure | 28<br>Criminal Law<br>& Procedure | 29<br>Makeup Time<br>9-11 am<br>Performance<br>Test 1-4 pm |
| 30 | July 1<br>Civil<br>Procedure | 2<br>Civil<br>Procedure | 3<br>Civil<br>Procedure | 4<br>Off | 5<br>Professional<br>Responsibility | 6<br>Wills<br>Trust |
| 7 | 8<br>Wills<br>&<br>Trusts | 9<br>Wills<br>&<br>Trusts | 10<br>Wills<br>&<br>Trusts | 11<br>Corporations | 12<br>Corporations | 13<br>Corporations |
| 14 | 15<br>Community<br>Property | 16<br>Community<br>Property | 17<br>Makeup<br>Time | 18<br>Makeup<br>Time | 19<br>SIM EXAM<br>all day | 20<br>SIM EXAM<br>all day |
| 21<br>Memorize | 22<br>Memorize | 23<br>Memorize | 24<br>Memorize | 25<br>Memorize | 26<br>Memorize | 27<br>Memorize |
| 28<br>Memorize | 29<br>Off | 30<br>Bar Exam | 31<br>Bar Exam | Aug 1<br>Bar Exam | 2 | 3 |

Notice I marked July 4 "OFF." There is no point in studying on a national holiday, so enjoy it. Also, the holiday comes at a time when you are switching from MBE subjects to non-MBE subjects, and provides a nice break.

Now it is time to calendar each day in each subject. Plan to write two essays a day, review your answers, compare them to the samples, and rewrite both essays. This will take you at least five hours, maybe six depending on your familiarity with the subject. You should expect the first draft of a one-hour essay to take more than an hour to write. You should also allow yourself to use your outline to answer the question. It is pointless to take an exam on a subject you haven't seen for three years without looking at the law. So use your outline to take practice exams. Write first drafts with your outline open, and rewrite with the outline shut, if you can.

Next, plan to take 15 multiple-choice questions, review, analyze, and record in writing why you missed them. Plan to take them in the morning one day and in the afternoon the next. Use the self-grading questionnaire for multiple-choice questions included at the end of this chapter to help you.

In four days, you will have taken five essays twice and answered 45 multiple-choice questions, without even using your evenings yet. Plan the rest of the subjects the same way. Here's an example from my bar calendar.

| MON | TUES | WED |
|---|---|---|
| 3 | 4 | 5 |
| Torts Remedies | Torts Remedies | Torts Remedies |
| 9 am–12 noon | 9 am–12 noon | 9 am–12 noon |
| write one new essay, review, rewrite | rewrite yesterday's exam | rewrite yesterday's exam |
| | write new exam | write new exam |
| | do 15 mult. choice review & analyse | review, rewrite exam |
| 2 pm-5 pm | 2 pm-5 pm | 2 pm-5 pm |
| exam | rewrite morning exam | do 15 mult. choice review & analyze |
| do 15 mult. choice review & analyse | write new one | |
| write new exam | | |
| 7 pm–9 pm makeup | 7 pm–9 pm makeup | 7 pm–9 pm makeup |

### 39. Be Reasonable and Flexible in Your Planning

Now that you have made this beautiful calendar, be reasonable and flexible when using it. For this reason, write it in pencil. You may find you need less time than you have allowed, or more. Adjust it accordingly. You will find that it needs adjusting at least once a week, maybe more.

You have more weeks to study for the February Bar Exam than the July Bar Exam, so you can spread out your preparation a bit more if need be. You should also mark December 24 to January 1 "OFF" for the same reason July 4 is marked "OFF" above.

### 40. Don't Abandon Your Plan

Now that you made this great plan, stick to it. This may seem contrary to the advice above, but it is not. You must strike a balance between flexibility and adherence. You can adjust your calendar if you get behind; however, you mustn't adjust it so much that the plan is of no use. If you get too far behind, use evenings, Saturday mornings, and Sundays to catch up.

### 41. Use Your Makeup Time for Just That

I guarantee you will get behind. It is the nature of the beast. Don't wait to finish every essay and multiple-choice question in a subject before moving on, or you will get so behind you won't be able to catch up. Spend your allotted time and do the rest during the evening or on Saturday or Sunday makeup sessions.

### 42. Prioritize, Prioritize, Prioritize

You will not know everything for the bar. It is not possible, nor are you expected to know everything. Learn the big concepts and some of the small ones and move on. Don't get stuck in the details. Focus on learning to problem-solve when you don't know what to do. Spend three to four days or so on a subject efficiently and effectively. Take six different exams that cover as many of the different issues in a given subject as possible. When your four days are up, move on! If you haven't finished, do the rest on a makeup day.

If you have a number of different things to do on a makeup day, do the material you find most difficult first. It doesn't further your goal of passing the bar exam to take exams or answer multiple-choice questions that are easy and that you already do well on.

Following this calendar is a good way to learn time management and strategies and tactics. You are learning to use your time for maximum benefit. Remember this test is about breadth, not depth, of knowledge.

### 43. Pace Yourself

You will notice that in the above illustration most of the study time is marked off in three-hour blocks, just as the test is given in three-hour blocks. However, this doesn't mean you should sit at your desk for three hours straight. You need to pace yourself and work up to that amount by breaking down those three-hour blocks of study time into manageable one-hour amounts. During each one-hour block, don't talk to anyone, daydream, or do anything other than write essays, answer multiple-choice questions, review answers, rewrite answers, etc. If you find your mind is straying, gently bring yourself back to the present. After your hour is up, no matter how much you have accomplished, break for 10 minutes. Repeat this process every hour for the next two. Then take a break for an hour or an hour and a half. Follow the same pattern in the afternoon.

This process of one-hour focused study followed by a 10-minute break accomplishes two things. First, it gets your body and mind accustomed to bar exam conditions, that is, sitting and staying focused. Second, it trains your body and mind to do what you ask of them. This is especially true of the mind. If you say to yourself that you will give yourself a break after one hour and then you don't, you've gone back on your word, and your mind registers this. Soon it will get so fed up, it will just stop cooperating. We've all had those days when we sit in the library all day, but get nothing done. This is because we've burned out our minds and haven't honored our promises to it.

So start honoring these promises. Once your mind understands that you are serious, it will be more cooperative when you need it to be.

### 44. Be The Tortoise, Not The Hare

Most of us grew up with the story of the tortoise. The tortoise and the hare agree to race. The hare is cocky and believes he will win. He starts out running, gets tired, and stops to rest, thinking the tortoise can never catch up with him. While he's sleeping, the tortoise slowly and methodically perseveres one step at a time. He doesn't stop to rest. He doesn't tire easily, because his pace is slow but steady. When the hare wakes up, he realizes he's behind and races to the finish line. However, it is too late because the tortoise has already crossed it.

I tell you this story because I see examples of it every day in my students. Most bar students behave like the hare. They attempt to study 10 to 12 hours a day every day from June 1 until the bar exam the last week in July. Inevitably, the pace becomes too much for them and they crash around July 4. They then stop studying, often for several days in a row, sometimes even up to a week. Next, they panic because they are now behind, and they frantically try to catch up in the remaining two weeks.

However, if you are the tortoise, this will not happen too you. If you are the tortoise, you work steadily six to eight hours a day six days a week, and take one day off a week. If you are doing the right things to prepare, if your study is efficient and effective, you only need six to eight hours a day. This means taking essays, reviewing them, rewriting them, answering multiple-choice questions, reviewing the questions you got wrong and understanding why, and taking performance tests.

### 45. Reward Yourself Every Day
Give yourself a little reward to work toward every day, such as a piece of chocolate, or a movie, or a walk in the park, or shopping, or watching a basketball or baseball game, or having a drink with your friends. Buy yourself a flower, a CD, a plant, a toy. It doesn't have to be big, but it has to be something you like. The point is to reward yourself daily in some way for getting your studying done. It will make it easier to do your work and make the study period more pleasant.

### 46. Stop Procrastinating!
According to the American Heritage Dictionary, procrastination is "to put off doing something, esp. out of habitual carelessness or laziness...." But my experience is that most students studying for the bar exam do not procrastinate because they are careless or lazy. You can't be careless or lazy and get through college and law school. Thus, procrastination is usually the product of anxiety and fear.

Procrastination, if unchecked, will raise your stress and worry levels to beyond tolerable and will ultimately sabotage your attempt to pass the bar exam. The way to stop procrastinating is to face the unknown. Write out why you are avoiding your studies and analyze your reasons. What do you fear? What about this test makes you feel anxious? Are you feeling overwhelmed? Obtaining answers to these questions and formulating a plan to address them will release you from procrastination. If you ignore the reasons you procrastinate or fail to address them once you recognize them, procrastination will sabotage your attempt to pass the bar exam.

## 47. Take Advantage of Every Moment

Students often tell me that by the time they did this or that, they only had an hour left to study, and they thought, why bother, it's not enough time. This is untrue. You can get a lot accomplished in an hour here or there. You can do 16 multiple-choice questions, review them for errors, and write up an analysis of your mistakes. You can write a whole essay exam. You can  rewrite an exam you already wrote. Don't let this be an excuse to avoid studying. Use every moment you have, even if it's less than an hour.

## 48. Prepare for the Unknown and Unexpected

An important step to keeping stress and worry from affecting your performance on the bar is preparing for the unknown and unexpected. Be prepared for the lights to go out in the exam room or for it to be too hot or too cold. Be prepared for an earthquake or other natural disaster. What if a person sitting near you gets sick during the exam? What if a person sitting near you doesn't come back from lunch or doesn't come back the next day? What would you do if these things were to happen?

Visit the site of the test. How much time will it take you to get there? What happens if public transportation isn't available? What if there is a traffic jam? Will you need a hotel? What about parking? Getting answers to these questions will lower your stress and worry levels, and you'll stay calm when and if the unexpected happens.

### 49. Make A Motivational Three-by-Five-Inch Card and Keep It On Your Desk

When I was studying for the bar exam, I kept a three-by-five-inch card on my desk with the following written on it in colorful ink:
**Me vs. the State Bar.**

Around these words, I drew a boxing ring:

**ME**

**VS.**

**THE STATE BAR**

This card reminded me of my purpose whenever my attention would stray from my studies. I would see the card and remember that I was in the boxing ring with the State Bar, and if I didn't pay attention I was going to get hit and go down. Every time my eye caught sight of the card after my mind had drifted away, I would say to myself, "I'm not going to give you a chance to hit me, State Bar," and I would go back to work. I highly recommend you make your own motivational card. You can use mine, or draw something of your own that expresses the goal, and that will motivate you when you drift off or just don't feel like studying.

# Chapter 10

# Improve Your Essay Writing Skills

The bar exam requires you to write essay answers to questions about hypothetical fact patterns on any number of legal subjects. The logical way to prepare for such a test would be to practice taking similar essay exams, and many of them at that. This is exactly what my students do to prepare. They take six exams in every subject covering a breadth of issues and they rewrite them all.

When I ask students who have failed the bar exam if they wrote practice exams, the answer is often "no" or "one or two in every subject." They spent their time memorizing the law.

The bar exam does test knowledge of the law, but more importantly, it tests your ability to explain it and apply it to different situations in an organized and easy-to-read fashion. You can't obtain this skill by memorizing and reviewing the law. The only way to obtain this skill is to write a first draft essay answer, review the sample answer, learn what you missed, and rewrite your answer. You learn a lot of law this way, in a context that makes sense (a fact pattern) instead of in a vacuum (out of an outline). More importantly, you are practicing what you will actually do in the bar exam itself.

When you study this way, by writing essays and rewriting them, you will find that your first drafts are often horrible. This is the nature of first drafts and instead of taking it personally understand that this is okay and as it should be. My first drafts were bad. I assure you that the first drafts of the essays the students in my bar review write are bad too. This is okay and part of the process.

## 50. Learn How to Write in IRAC Form

The bar examiners expect you to write your essays in IRAC form. IRAC stands for issue, rule, analysis or application, and conclusion. Every law student has heard of it, but many don't know what it means to write this way, and as a consequence will fail the bar exam. When properly followed, IRAC form quickly demonstrates to the grader that you know what you're doing. The grader has already taken the bar exam and passed it, and thus knows how to write in IRAC form.

When I'm reading a blue book I expect to see the issue in a heading, and I expect to see the rule follow the issue heading. When it doesn't, I get a bad feeling about the essay, because I know I will have to hunt through the essay looking for the student's rules and analysis. In short, I will have to work very hard to see if the student did what he or she was supposed to do. However, when you write in IRAC form, it is very easy for graders to follow your logic, which makes their job easy. As a result, they will bend over backwards to try to give you a passing grade.

One of the best ways to obtain the perspective of the grader is to grade. I make my students grade each other's exams. They quickly see that it is a tedious and boring task, which can be made harder by a disorganized answer not written in IRAC form, or easier by an organized answer that is. Remember, graders are grading hundreds of blue books. After the first 10 or so, they know what they want to see and what it should look like. If yours doesn't look like that, you make it harder for the grader to pass you.

Here's how to write IRAC. First, put the issue in a heading. Follow the issue heading with a rule of law that governs that issue. In a new paragraph, write your analysis; that is, apply the facts to the elements of the law. A good analysis contains fact, law, and an explanation of how the facts do or do not meet the elements of the law. Finally, write your conclusion, and do so in a way that a) makes sense and b) moves you to the next issue.

## 51. Answer the Self-Grading Essay Exam Questionnaire

One of the best ways to learn IRAC is to take an exam and then answer my Self-Grading Essay Exam Questionnaire included in this book. I developed this questionnaire after a frustrating day teaching first year law students who were on probation. I was not getting through to them about IRAC, and the semester was rapidly ending. I realized that they weren't improving because they didn't know what questions to ask about their own work, the questions I ask about their work when I grade it. I promptly sat down and wrote these questions down in detail.

The next week I handed the students their exams from the previous week, along with a sample answer and my questionnaire. I told the class they were going to learn how to grade their own exams by filling out the questionnaire. The only other direction I gave was that they were not to answer any of the questions with just a yes or no answer.

The next week, although the students complained about how much time the questionnaire took to fill out, they all said they learned a lot about IRAC and essay-writing by filling it out. Their work reflected this as well. Their subsequent essays were much better, and they all had better awareness of what they were doing wrong and how to fix it.

The questionnaire proved so helpful that I use it in all my classes now, both law school and bar review. The student taking it not only learns essay-writing skill, but gains self-reliance. The questions help you figure out what you're doing right and what you are doing wrong, which is very empowering. This empowerment leads to confidence, which in turn lowers stress and worry and thus greatly increases your chances of passing the bar exam.

On the next page is the questionnaire:

# SELF-GRADING QUESTIONNAIRE
# FOR LAW SCHOOL AND BAR EXAMS

After taking an exam, do the exercises below and answer the questions as specifically and thoroughly as you can. (Yes or no answers without further explanation will not suffice.) Actively filling out this form will help you identify your problem areas and improve them.

**A.** After reading the sample answer, create an Issue List by listing on a separate piece of paper each issue in the sample answer in the order it was discussed. (Leave a couple of blank lines between each. You will need them later.) For example, the Issue List of a Negligence fact pattern might look like this:

## ISSUE LIST OF SAMPLE ANSWER
Negligence
Duty
Foreseeable plaintiff
Standard of Care
Breach
Actual Cause
Proximate Cause
Damages
Contributory Negligence
Comparative Negligence

On another piece of paper, make a list of the issues from your answer. Compare the two lists and answer the following questions:

1. How many of the issues in the sample answer did I miss?
2. Were the issues I missed big (i.e. major issues requiring lots of analysis and possibly counter arguments) or small (requiring little analysis)? List the major and minor issues you missed.
3. As to each issue, did I write more or less analysis, than the sample answer? Was it necessary to write more than the sample answer? If I wrote less, what did I miss?
4. Did I discuss the issues in the same order as the answer? If not, was my order logical? If not, in what order should I have discussed the issues?

**B.** Next, write each rule from the sample answer under the appropriate issue on the sample answer Issue List. Here's an example of what it would look like if you were analyzing a sample answer for a Negligence fact pattern:

## ISSUE AND LAW LIST OF SAMPLE ANSWER

### Negligence (Issue)

In order to prove negligence plaintiff must prove its elements. They are duty, breach, causation, and damages. (Rule)

### Duty

To prove that the defendant owed a duty to plaintiff, plaintiff must prove that he or she was a foreseeable plaintiff.

### Foreseeable Plaintiff

According to Cardozo, a foreseeable plaintiff is one in the zone of danger of defendant's act. The Andrews view is that everyone is a foreseeable plaintiff.

### Standard of Care

Landowners have a duty to those hurt by artificial conditions that start on the land and go off the land.

### Breach

A defendant has breached his duty to plaintiff when his behavior falls below the applicable standard of care.

### Actual Cause

But for the defendant's negligent act, plaintiff would not have been hurt

### Proximate Cause

The defendant is liable for all harm he directly caused and all foreseeable harm from his actions.

### Damages

Plaintiff must suffer damage in order to recover.

You have now created an Issue and Law List of the sample answer. Next highlight all the rules you wrote in your answer. For each rule, you wrote ask the following questions.

1. Is the rule I wrote the same as the one in the sample answer?

2. If not, what is it missing?

3. Is the rule I wrote correct? Is it complete?

4. Have I written the rule in a way that I can easily apply facts to it?

5. If not, how can I re-write this rule so I can?

6. Did I miss a rule?

C. Next, locate the fact or facts used to prove (or disprove) each element of each rule in the sample answer. Write these facts next to the appropriate element of each rule on your Issue and Law List.

For example:
**Foreseeable Plaintiff**
According to Cardozo, a foreseeable plaintiff is one in the zone of danger of defendant's act.

The elements of this rule are:
> **Defendant**
> **Defendant's act**
> **Zone of Danger**
> **Foreseeable Plaintiff**

---

**Defendant** = Jack.
**Defendant's Act** = Jack racing his motorcycle across his property onto a public road.
**Zone of Danger** =property and public road.
**Foreseeable Plaintiff** = Peter.
**Foreseeable** = because he was on the road when Jack raced across it.

With a pen, circle each analysis section in your own answer. For each circled section ask the following questions:
1. Does each element of the rule appear next to facts and explanation?
2. Did I explain how the facts meet the elements so that a grader who doesn't know the facts or law would understand it?
3. Did I use the appropriate facts for each element?
4. Did I analyze all the elements of the rule with facts?
5. Did I discuss each element in the order it was listed in the rule above?
6. Did I use more facts than necessary to prove the rule?
7. Did I use irrelevant facts in my analysis?

8. Did I repeat an analysis of an element of the rule?
9. Did I write any sentences that only contain facts? If so, were they followed with and explanation of how they meet the rule?
10. Did I analyze elements other than what were part of the rule?

D. Next, read your answer aloud and ask yourself the following questions:
   1. Does each paragraph logically follow to the next? If not, where does it break down? Why does it break down there?
   2. Does each sentence logically follow to the next? If not, where do they not follow and why?
   As you read each sentence ask the following questions:
   3. Does this sentence make sense?
   4. Is this sentence concise?
   5. Is this a full sentence?
   6. Is this sentence relevant to the issue above it?
   7. Does this sentence repeat what I wrote earlier?
   8. Does this sentence contradict what I wrote earlier?

E Next to each sentence identify with the letters I, R, A, C what part of IRAC each represents and answer the following questions:
   1. Are any of the sentences not representative of some part of IRAC? How many?
   2. Are any of the sentences out of IRAC order? Mark every place that the sentences are out of IRAC order.
   3. Is there an analysis for every rule stated?

F Next, look at your exam as a whole and answer the following questions:
   1. Did you finish the exam?
   2. If no, why not?
   3. Did you spend too much time on small issues?
   4. Did you spend time on non-issues?
   5. Did you apportion your time appropriately?
   6. Did you plan your time effectively before you wrote your answer?
   7. Did I answer the question or questions asked?

G. Finally, re-write the exam using the Issue and Law List you created. (You've already written 60% of it because this list contains all the issues and all the rules of the sample answer. All you have to do is write the analysis.)

## 51. Be Proactive about Reviewing and Rewriting

The questionnaire requires that you be proactive in the process of reviewing and rewriting. The more specific your answers are to the questions in the questionnaire, and the more you fill it out, the more you'll improve. It will not help you to complain that this is too hard, or to respond with yes or no answers, or to skip some of the questions. However, if you are proactive and make the effort to objectively review your work the way a grader will, by thoroughly and thoughtfully answering the questions on the questionnaire, you will improve.

## 52. Follow Instructions Carefully

After not writing in the IRAC form, one of the primary reasons students fail the bar exam is they don't follow instructions. The instructions are very specific. The grader wants only certain issues discussed. It is your job to figure out what is required and write it and only it. If you write about the whole sink, when all that was asked for was the faucet, you won't pass, and you'll annoy the grader.

## 53. Practice, Practice, Practice

Take six to eight practice exams in every multistate subject (Torts, Contracts, Real Property, Constitutional Law, Criminal Law, Criminal Procedure, and Evidence) and rewrite them all. Take four to five in each nonmultistate subject and rewrite them all as well. (In California, these subjects are Civil Procedure, Professional responsibility, Wills, Trusts, Community Property, Corporations, and Remedies.)

## 54. Plan before You Write

When I write a paper, I write down all my thoughts in whatever order they come to me in the first draft, and then I move the paragraphs and sentences around so that they flow logically in my second draft. However, you don't have time to do this on a one-hour essay exam on the bar exam. You have to use an outline to plan and organize your answer before you write it in one draft.

Your essay is your job interview to practice law. If you don't plan and organize your answer before you write it, you will have an essay full of cross-outs and inserts. The prose will not flow in an organized manner from one paragraph to the next, or from one sentence to the next. This will frustrate the grader, who will not be able to understand what you are trying to say. If they can't follow you, they can't pass you.

Now I know that outlining feels awkward at best for many students. However, it can be learned. The first step is to read the call of the question to ascertain what subject is being tested. Below is a fact pattern. Find the call, read it, and see if you can determine what subject is being tested.

> One evening, at approximately 6:30, Susan, a newly sworn-in attorney, was happily walking down the street when she saw a lovely strain of pearls in Calvetti's Jewelry shop window. Susan thought how nice it would be to have the pearls to celebrate her recent bar passage, but knew she couldn't afford them, since she had spent all her savings on law school and bar exam preparation.
>
> "I think I'll steal them," she thought. Susan then noticed the window behind which the pearls lay was open about six inches. She put her hand through the opening, and just before she touched them, she changed her mind, because she was afraid she would jeopardize her state bar license and career as an attorney. She then withdrew her hand and continued walking down the street.

### What crime, if any, has Susan committed?

This one was easy: **criminal law**. However, sometimes the call of the question doesn't reveal much, so in that case you have to read the fact pattern before you can go further. Here, since you know that criminal law is being tested you can go to the next step: write down your criminal law approach outline on the left side of a piece of scratch paper.

Your criminal law approach outline should contain a list of all the issues tested in criminal law, organized in a logical manner. Your approach outline is the ultimate reduction of your long outline of the subject, which should contain all the rules of criminal law written in **full sentences** just as you would write them on an exam. My criminal law approach outline looks like this:

I.   Jurisdiction

II.  Merger

III. **Elements**
     A. Act
     B. Mental State

IV.  **Accomplice Liability**

V.   **Inchoate Offenses**
     A. Solicitation
     B. Conspiracy
     C. Attempt with defenses

VI.  **Criminal Capacity**
     A. Insanity
     B. Intoxication
     C. Infancy
     D. Defenses
             Insanity
             Drink
             Entrapment
             Mistake
             Age
             Necessity
             Duress
             Crime Prevention
             Other
             Property
             Self

VII. **Offenses against People**
     A. Battery
     B. Assault
     C. Mayhem
     D. False Imprisonment
     E. Kidnapping
     F. Homicide
             1. Murder
                a. malice
             2. First degree
             3. Second degree
             4. Felony Murder
             5. Manslaughter
                b. voluntary
                c. involuntary
             6. Causation

VIII. **Sex Offenses**
     A. Rape
             1. Statutory
             2. Bestiality

IX.  **Property Offenses**
     A. Larceny
     B. Larceny by Trick
     C. Embezzlement
     D. False Pretense
     E. Robbery
     F. Extortion
     G. Receiving Stolen Property

X.   **Offenses against Habitation**
     A. Burglary
     B. Arson

Across the top of the scratch paper write the call of the question or questions. Next, read the fact pattern. This is your first read, after which you can determine what area in the approach outline the examiners are testing. Here, they are testing Burglary. Now read the fact pattern again, this time line by line, word by word, placing facts next to the appropriate elements of the rule in your approach outline. This is what your approach outline should look like now:

### X. Offenses against Habitation      <u>Susan's Crimes</u>
Common Law Burglary
Breaking—*no, window open six inches*
and entering—*yes, "she put her hand through the opening"*
Of a dwelling of another—*no, Calvetti's Jewelry shop, commercial*
At night—*6:30? Might be night, might not, depends on time of year*
With intent to commit a felony therein—*"I think I'll steal them" referring to pearls. Conclusion: no burglary at common law because no breaking, not a dwelling, and may not be at night.*

Modern law—*Yes, burglary met because it doesn't have to be a dwelling, also doesn't have to be at night. Also only need entering, don't need breaking.*

Notice how I don't just write yes or no next to each element. I write in all the nitty-gritty specific facts I need to prove the element and to write a thorough analysis. Now read the call and the fact pattern for any missed facts and ask yourself whether they trigger any other issues in your list. (I have purposely used only a part of a hypothetical here for an example. There, of course, would be other issues and possibly other calls.)

The last step is time management. You guess at how much time each issue or cluster of issues will take to write and apportion your time accordingly. The more facts surrounding an issue, the longer it will take to write about.

For a one-hour exam, you should allow 12-15 minutes to outline and apportion your time, and 45 minutes for writing. For other time allotments, allocate 20 to 25% of the time for outlining and apportioning time, and the rest for writing your answer.

Outlining will help you stay organized, identify all the issues, and write an exam free of cross-outs and inserts. In addition, outlining will help you determine what counter-arguments to make and when to make them. Outlining will also help you manage your time so that you give each issue the appropriate weight and finish in time.

# Chapter 11

# Improve Your Multiple Choice Skills

### 55. Improve Your Multiple Choice Skills

I find that many students have a "thing" about multiple-choice questions, much like a hatred of math. I, too, was never very good at them throughout school and on the SAT and LSAT, but had to learn them for the bar exam. In the process of learning how to do them, I found that my hatred of them interfered with my ability to accurately answer them because my focus was split between avoiding my anxiety about multiple-choice questions and answering the question.

To counter this, every time I thought about how much I hated multiple-choice questions, I stopped the thought and instead told myself, "Don't love them, don't hate them, just do them." This kept me focused on the question instead of the how I felt about them and I started answering more accurately. Thus, whenever you tell yourself "Oh, I hate multiple-choice questions," stop and instead say, "Don't love them, don't hate them, just do them."

### 56. Test Your Reading Comprehension Skills

You need to have solid reading comprehension skills to perform well on multiple-choice questions. This is because the questions are very precise. The better you understand the call of the question, the fact pattern, and the answers, the more likely you are to answer correctly.

The problem is that many students read the questions the same way they read the newspaper: the information just passes through them and doesn't stick. You can test yourself to see if you read like this. Read the call of the question (that's the question located at the end of the fact pattern) and cover it immediately after you've read it. Then try to explain aloud exactly what it asked. I make my students do this exercise, and most of them cannot recall what they just read. You can't read like this and perform well on multiple choice questions. You must know exactly what the call is asking for at all times. If you don't, there is little chance you will correctly answer the question.

## 57. Multiple-Choice Approach
Here's my approach to answering multiple-choice questions.

1. Read the call of the question
The call of the question is located at the bottom of the fact pattern before the answers. The number one reason students answer multiple-choice questions incorrectly is that they don't choose the answer that is most responsive to the call. This is often because they haven't understood the precise thing the call of the question asked for. You must know what the question is in order to answer it correctly.

2. Recall the call of the question
Cover the call of the question and ask yourself what you just read. If you can't remember what you just read, then you don't really understand the question. Go back and read it again. You should be able to accurately summarize what the call asked you after you've read it.

3. Read the fact pattern
Keeping the call of the question in your head, read the fact pattern. As you read each paragraph, ask yourself, "Does this paragraph help me answer the question asked?" This technique is very helpful in eliminating unnecessary facts, and it speeds up the process of getting to the right answer.

4. Read the call and eliminate two answers
Summon the applicable legal test or rule and apply it to the facts. Using this analysis, eliminate two answers. Most people get this far. The trick is in the next round.

5. Look for the fact or facts that make the difference
Read the call of the question, the two remaining answers, and relevant sections of the fact pattern again, looking for a fact or two that makes one answer more responsive to the call of the question than the other. Apply the facts to the applicable test and reason out the correct answer. Choose and move on.

## 58. Manage Your Time

You have 1.8 minutes per question and three hours to do 100 questions. This means you must complete approximately 16 questions every 30 minutes, or 33 every hour. You need a time management strategy that will help you get enough questions done in each half hour so that you won't get so far behind you can't catch up. I write the time I need to have completed each set of 16 questions next to the appropriate number.

For example, if your exam begins at 9 AM and you know that 16 questions must be completed in a half hour, put "9:30" next to number 16. You also know that 33 questions must be completed in one hour, so next put "10" next to number 33. Continue counting and writing times in this manner until you've allotted three hours. Then, as you analyze each question, you can watch the time and push to complete the set by the half-hour mark. Each question is worth the same amount of points, so don't ruminate too long on any one. It isn't worth it.

## 59. Practice without Time Pressure for the First Four Weeks

Students tend to try to do too much all at once. They expect to score 70% in the time allotted at the beginning of the study period, although it has been three years since they've reviewed much of the law tested on the bar exam. This is like expecting a child who has just learned to walk to run a marathon. You haven't seen these subjects in two to three years, so cut yourself some slack.

Do 12-15 per day without time pressure for the first four weeks of study when you are reviewing the subjects for the first time. During this time, perfect your method and learn the law. After you have reviewed all the subjects tested, add the time pressure and do 33 in an hour every other day.

## 60. Emphasize Quality over Quantity

You needn't do 2,000 questions. Remember, you are only going to have 33 in every subject, except Torts and Contracts, in which there are 34. If you did 100 in every subject, you will have taken approximately three times the number you will actually have on the exam. If you practice 200, then you have completed six times the number tested on the bar exam. That is more than enough if you do them thoughtfully. (For more about how to do this, see Identify Your Mistakes below.)

My students take 12-15 multiple-choice questions per day for the first four weeks of the study period. When we review Torts, they write essays and answer multiple-choice questions in Torts. When we review Contracts, they write essays and answer multiple-choice questions in Contracts. And so forth. The small number of questions allows time for them to methodically assess their mistakes and learn from them. During this time, they learn a lot of law, as well as test-taking skills.

In the last four weeks of study, my students answer 33 questions in one hour every other day. By this time they have learned the law, have perfected their skill, and are ready for the additional challenge of time management. At the end of the study period, they take a simulated exam of 100 questions. The total number of questions taken by each student in my course is approximately 900 to 1,000 questions.

### 61. Identify Your Mistakes

This is crucial to improving your performance. Every season students call me saying that they answered 2,000 multiple-choice questions when studying, and they still failed the MBE portion of the bar exam. This is because they did not practice them thoughtfully. They did the questions by rote, and did not stop to figure out and understand why they missed questions.

To solve this problem, I require my students to write up an analysis of their mistakes in a notebook and chart them as well. (Below is a sample of both.) If you don't know why you're missing the questions, you can't improve.

**#28** Woman buys a stove with a warning on <u>the crate</u> that it will tip over if 25 lbs or more is set on its oven door. Woman's 3 year old climbed on the oven door to see what's cooking and the stove tips—child burned.
<u>-Woman sues local retailer in strict liability</u>.

**Issue**: straight strict products liability elements question.

**Rule:** To hold a retailer liable for strict liability, plaintiff must show:

**1. Defect**: product in a defective condition, that it is unreasonably dangerous to the user/consumer  — Here, stove door defective.

**2. Control:** The condition must have existed when it left the defendant's control. Here, condition existed when left local retailer's store cause label warned would tip over if more than 25 pounds on it.

**3. Changes:** The product must not be expected to undergo significant changes before it gets to the user (or, it must not undergo significant changes.) Here, didn't change at local retailer.

**4. Business:** The seller must be in the business of selling the product. Here, local retailer sold stoves.

**5. Causation**: Damage must result from defect. Here, defective door couldn't hold the weight of the child, tipped and burned child.

**6. Privity:** No privity required.

**What I did wrong?**: I chose answer A: that Local Retailer did not inform mother of warning on the crate. However, don't necessarily have to prove failure to warn by local retailer in order to prevail—not one of the elements. I also didn't know element number 3 of the rule which was the only answer that was available that precisely answered the question.

**Answer:** The woman has to establish that the stove was substantially in the same condition at the time it tipped over as when it was purchased from the local retailer.

After looking at this example, a student drafted the following chart to use in addition to the notebook, so that he could see at a glance if there was a pattern to the questions he missed. Below is a revised version of his chart for your use.

SUBJECT:

QUESTIONS FROM:

| ISSUE TESTED | # | MISREAD THE CALL OF THE QUESTION | CHOSE ANSWER THAT MIS-REPRESENTED THE FACTS | CHOSE ANSWER THAT WAS LEGALLY WRONG | DIDN'T KNOW THE LAW | APPLIED THE LAW WRONG | DIDN'T CHOOSE THE MOST PRECISE ANSWER |
|---|---|---|---|---|---|---|---|
| | | | | | | | |
| | | | | | | | |
| | | | | | | | |
| | | | | | | | |
| | | | | | | | |
| | | | | | | | |
| | | | | | | | |
| | | | | | | | |
| | | | | | | | |
| | | | | | | | |
| | | | | | | | |
| | | | | | | | |
| | | | | | | | |
| | | | | | | | |
| | | | | | | | |
| | | | | | | | |
| | | | | | | | |

You can also use the multiple-choice questionnaire below to help you identify why you are missing questions. Also, there is a great book entitled STRATEGIES AND TACTICS FOR THE MBE, published by Emanuel Publishing Corp. The book has great answer explanations, general multiple-choice strategies, specific strategies for each, and a good list of why answers are wrong. I highly recommend it.

## SELF-GRADING QUESTIONNAIRE
## FOR MULTIPLE-CHOICE QUESTIONS ON LAW SCHOOL EXAMS AND THE MULTISTATE BAR EXAM

After taking a series of practice multiple-choice questions and reviewing their answers, for each question you missed do the exercises below and answer the questions as specifically and thoroughly as you can. (Yes or no answers without further explanation will not suffice.)   Actively filling out this form will help you identify your problems with multiple-choice questions and improve them.

I. Write the number of the multiple-choice question and the book it came from on a separate sheet of paper.

II. Write the general subject matter tested (for example, Contracts) and the specific issue that was tested (for example Offer).

III. Briefly summarize the fact pattern and call of the question.

IV. Write down the correct answer and your answer choice. Using the problem and the answer's explanation as a guide, answer the following questions:
  1. Did I miss this question because of the rule?
  2. Did I choose an answer in which the law was wrong?
  3. Did I choose an answer that overstated the elements of a crime, tort, or admissibility of evidence?
  4. Did I choose an answer that used an antiquated rule or rule from an inapplicable body of law?
  5. Did I choose an answer that used a rule that didn't apply to these facts?

V. Write out the correct rule needed to answer this question.

1. Did I miss this question because of the facts?

2. Did I misread the facts? Did I miss a fact important to the answer?

3. Did I choose an answer in which the reasoning mischaracterized the facts? If so, did the facts in the answer contradict the facts in the problem? If not, did the answer I chose go beyond the facts in the problem? If not, did I choose an answer that assumed a fact in dispute?

4. Did I choose an answer that applied the law correctly to the facts?

5. Did I choose the most precise or effective answer? Of the two possible correct answer choices, did I choose the one that was more difficult to prove? (Choose the one that is easier to prove in that situation.) Did I choose the less precise answer?

6. Did I truly understand the call of the question when I was reading the fact pattern? Did I truly understand the call of the question when I answered it? When taking your next multiple-choice test, after reading the call of the question, cover it and ask yourself, "What was I asked to do?" If you can't answer this question accurately, you don't understand the call well enough to choose the correct answer.

7. Did I have any feelings about the characters involved while answering the question? (For example, often students will feel sorry for a character who got hurt in the fact pattern, and will want to choose an answer that finds for him or her even if the answer doesn't precisely respond to the call of the question.) If so, did these feelings affect my judgment?

8. Did I have any feelings about the material tested while answering this question? (If you hate a subject, such as property, and you think, "I hate property" while you're answering the question, your focus is split between avoiding your anxiety about property and answering the question, making it more likely you will choose the wrong answer.) Did my feelings about the subject matter affect my judgment?

9. Did I have any feelings about the answer choices themselves? (Some students will get angry because the answer choice that they believe is the true answer isn't available to choose, and this will prevent them from choosing the answer that most precisely answers the call.) Did my feelings about the answer choices affect my judgment?

## 62. Don't Get Attached to the Parties
## or to Choosing the "Right" Answer

It is very important when answering multiple-choice questions not to get attached to the parties or to choosing the absolute "right" answer. If you are attached to the parties or to choosing the right answer, you will inevitably be swayed by this attachment and answer incorrectly. Remember, the parties aren't real, and the "right" answer is just the best of four usually bad ones.

I see the first kind of attachment in students all the time, especially women. Someone in the fact pattern gets hurt and the student feels bad and wants the person to win. So the student chooses the answer that awards damages even though it is wrong. To all of you who do this, keep in mind that the characters in these questions ARE NOT REAL. This will help you stay objective and not get pulled in emotionally.

The second kind of attachment is to choosing the "right" answer. This happens when the student summons the applicable test, applies the law to it, arrives at the "right" answer, but can't find it in the four choices. At this point, the student usually becomes frustrated and sometimes angry. It is this frustration and anger that can keep you from staying flexible and reasoning your way to the best choice of the available answers or to the three wrong answers.

## 63. Stop Looking for the Right Answer--Look for Three Wrong Ones

Instead of looking for the right answer, which is often not one of the choices, look for the three answers you know are wrong. This will help you detach from the "right" answer and not care why the one that is left after you have eliminated the wrong ones is the correct answer. Ultimately, it doesn't matter why the remaining answer is correct, because it is just a test.

## 64. Expect to Miss 50% in Practice

Expect to miss 50% until a week and a half before the bar. The learning curve for answering multiple-choice questions is very slow. It takes a long time to learn to do them accurately in the short amount of time allowed (1.8 minutes per question). So it is better to do fewer and do them daily than to do more all on one day of the week.

## 65. Celebrate Your Wrong Answers

It is demoralizing to practice multiple-choice questions and miss 50% each time you do them. This feeling can easily get to you and make you stop practicing them. I know it got to me. This is why you must change that feeling around so that you don't get discouraged. I tell my students that they should throw a mini-celebration every time they answer a question incorrectly. I tell them to say to themselves, "That is one more that I'll get right on the test." Better to miss them now, when you can learn from your mistakes, than to miss them on the bar exam. So celebrate every time you answer incorrectly. Your mood will improve and so will your scores.

## 66. Pick a Letter of the Day

Before you go into the test, choose your letter of the day. Whenever you decide to skip a question, automatically select the answer corresponding to this letter. By doing this, you have an automatic 25% chance of getting the question right with little time invested. Without the letter of the day strategy, a student who wishes to skip a question often chooses an answer by counting how many a, b, c, and d answers he has already chosen, and chooses an answer based on which one he has chosen the least often so far. This approach assumes your answer choices are all correct and that there are an equal number of a, b c, and d answers on the test. So don't waste time with this nonsense. Pick your letter of the day, any letter, and use it **every** time you skip.

## 67. Skipping Questions and the Horrible Scantron

At this writing, the multistate bar examiners are still using the Scantron form, kin to the butterfly ballot. It is terribly easy to fill in the wrong bubble because they are quite small and hard to read. So when you skip a question **always** use your letter of the day to answer that question on the Scantron. This way, you won't accidentally mark your answer for the next question in one of the bubbles for the skipped question. There's nothing worse than realizing in the middle of or at the end of a multiple-choice exam that your answers are all off by one number.

## 68. Use Multiple-Choice Questions to Learn the Minutiae

Multiple-choice questions test minutiae such as riparian water rights. They test the distinctions in the law (e.g. the UCC rules versus the common law rules in contracts) and the subrules of bigger concepts (e.g. proximate cause in Negligence) and the exceptions to the rule (e.g. exceptions to the Hearsay rule). Practicing multiple-choice questions is a great way to learn little rules and distinctions.

## 69. Use the Questionnaire, Notebook and Chart Diligently

Use the questionnaire, notebook, and chart diligently to learn from your mistakes. It does you no good to take them and miss them if you don't know why. The only way to increase your score is to figure out why you are missing.

## 70. Don't Love Them, Don't Hate Them

Many students come to me openly disliking Real Property, especially for Real Property multiple-choice questions. To them and to you I say, don't love them, don't hate them. You should not have strong emotions either way about multiple-choice questions in any subject. (This goes for essays too.) When you have strong feelings of liking a subject or hating it, you set yourself up to answer incorrectly. Strong emotions either way cloud judgment. Their presence blocks objectivity and reasoning, making it likely that you will miss important clues pointing toward the correct answer. So don't love 'em and don't hate 'em, just do 'em.

# Chapter 12

# Improve Your Performance Test Skills

You will feel much calmer about the performance test if you improve your skills. To improve, take sample performance tests and figure out if you did them correctly, and if not, why not. Since this is a book primarily on handling stress and worry, I've included an abbreviated version of the performance test approach I teach to my students. For a more specific approach, browse your local legal bookstore for books that discuss in depth the skills needed to pass the bar.

### 71. Perfect Your Approach to the Performance Test

1. Read the task section of the partner memo located at the end of the memo. Identify the skills tested by each task. Are they asking for fact gathering skills? Fact analysis skills? Legal analysis skills? Strategy and Tactics? Ethics? Do they want you to write a persuasive or objective document?

2. Next, make an outline of each task on a separate sheet of paper. You must read every word of the instructions and think about what they mean. You cannot read them the way you might read a newspaper, just gathering the general gist of an article. You must think about each word and sentence. If you have read the instructions carefully, you should be able to summarize in detail what you were asked to do and draft a skeleton of what each document will ultimately look like. If you can't do this, you haven't read the tasks carefully enough.

3. Read the partner memo from the beginning. As you read, think about how its contents relate to the tasks you were asked to perform. Add to your skeleton outline any facts you learned form the partner memo.

4. Keeping in mind what you were asked to do in the partner memo, read the library. If you find yourself reading a case and you don't know why, go back to the partner memo and figure out what you were asked to do. Then, return to the library, and after reading each paragraph ask yourself how this paragraph helps you perform the tasks you were asked to do. Take notes to the side of each paragraph. Every note you write and every word you underline should have something to do with solving the problem in the task memo. If you read each case with purpose, then what's important will stand out and what isn't will fall away. Your reading will be effective and time efficient.

5. After reading each case, write a short summary at the top of the page stating what the case stood for, whether it was for you or against you, its holding, and a brief summary of the facts. By reading this way, you will have synthesized the law—that is, you will know it so well you'll remember it and be able to apply it to the facts when reading the file.

6. Next, read the file. As you read the file, constantly ask yourself, how does what I am reading help solve the problem? Where do these facts fit with the law I've just read and the documents I was asked to write? Do they help me answer the question or not? If you do this, the facts that are important will stand out and those that aren't will fall away. Write a brief note next to each relevant fact about how it will be used.

7. Go back to your skeleton outline. Add to these "bones" short summaries of fact and law from your file and library. In your skeleton outline, note the page where you can find these items. Think about what you're going to write in each paragraph. There should be a representation of the substance of each paragraph on your skeleton outline.

8. Check to see if you truly answered the question asked. Read the task memo again. Ask yourself, does my skeleton represent what I was asked to do? Fix it if it doesn't.

9. Each task is assigned a percentage value—for example, the first task might be worth 60% and the second task might be worth 40%. Manage your time so that you do not spend more time on a task than it is worth.

### 72. Self-Grade Your Performance Tests

Use the self-grading questionnaire enclosed to grade your exams. This will help you identify your problems and correct them. Answer the questions thoroughly and honestly.

## SELF-GRADING QUESTIONNAIRE
## FOR PERFORMANCES EXAMS

After taking a performance exam, do the exercises below and answer the questions as specifically and thoroughly as you can. (Yes or no answers without further explanation will not suffice.) Actively filling out this form will help you identify your problem areas and improve them.

1. Read the sample answer carefully. On a separate sheet of paper, write all the headings in the sample answer in the order in which they occur. Briefly and thoroughly, summarize each paragraph from the sample answer under its appropriate heading. Next, read the partner memo's specific instructions, generally located on the second page and labeled A and B or 1 and 2. Notice how the sample answer mirrors the organization given to you in the specific instructions in the partner memo or in the form file. (If there is a second sample answer to the test, do the same analysis for it as well.)

2. Read your answer carefully. On a separate sheet of paper, write all the headings you used in the order in which they occur and answer the following questions:
   a. Are they the same or similar to the sample answer?
      If not, why not?
   b. Did you misread the partner instructions?
   c. Did you focus on the wrong issues?

3. Briefly and thoroughly summarize each paragraph in your answer, place it under its appropriate heading, and answer the following questions:
   a. Does your answer mirror the organization given to you in the specific instructions in the partner memo or in the form file? If no, why not?
   b. Is the content of each of your paragraphs the same as that in the sample answer? If not, why not?
   c. Did you discuss all the cases?

d. Did you distinguish cases that were against us? If so, did you distinguish based on the law or the facts?

e. Did you have the same or similar discussion or analysis as the sample answer? If not, why not?

4. If the skill tested was fact gathering (investigation plan, discovery plan), did you miss facts that should have been gathered?

a. Did your answer contain headings?

b. Were you expansive and thorough in what you requested to be gathered?

c. Were you specific about what you wanted, why you wanted it, and where it could be found?

5. If the skill was fact analysis (opening and closing statements, jury instructions, declarations and affidavits), did you miss facts that should have been analyzed?

a. Did your answer contain headings? (None required if it was a declaration or affidavit.)

b. Was it logically organized (in most cases chronologically)?

c. Did you adopt the correct tone—that is, did you adapt your writing to your audience. If you were writing to an investigator, did you explain what you were saying in lay person's terms without condescension? If you were writing an opening statement to a jury, was your tone pleasant and persuasive, instead of the argumentative tone of a closing statement?

6. If the skill was objective legal analysis (memo to the partner, client, opposing counsel), did you objectively analyze the problem?

a. Did your paragraphs follow the IRAC formula ( i.e. the first paragraph summarizes the law, the second paragraph explains the case the law came from and how the court applied the law to the facts in it, the third paragraph applies our specific facts to the law and explains how a court would rule, even if it is against us)?

b. If it was a memo to the partner, did you have an "issues presented" section and a "brief answer" section?

c. If it was a letter to the client or opposing counsel, did you adopt the correct tone?

7. If the skill was persuasive legal analysis, did you write persuasively?
   a. Are the paragraphs organized in the IRAC formula?
   b. Are your point headings specific to the laws and facts? Do they contain fact, law, and explanation in an argument form?
   c. Did you adopt the correct tone? Watch out for sarcasm and meanness.
8. Did you catch the ethical problem, if there was one?
9. Did you catch the strategic problem, if there was one?
10. Did you use common sense?
11. Next, read your answer aloud and ask yourself the following questions:
   a. Does each paragraph logically flow to the next?
      If not, where does it break down? Why does it break down there?
   b. Does each sentence logically flow to the next?
      If not, where do they not flow and why?
12. As you read each sentence, ask the following questions:
   a. Does this sentence make sense?
   b. Is this sentence concise?
   c. Is this a full sentence?
   d. Does this sentence logically follow the one above it?
   e. Is this sentence relevant to the heading that it follows?
   f. Does this sentence repeat what I wrote earlier?
   g. Does this sentence contradict what I wrote earlier?

## 73. Take Practice Tests

You must practice taking performance tests to improve your skills so that you can perform at your peak under pressure. You should write at least five during the study period, and outline in detail two more.

## A Final Note

In this book, I've tried to include everything I know about how to keep stress and worry from affecting your performance on the bar exam. If you diligently practice these tips, you can gain a great deal of relief from them, not only on the bar exam, but in your career as well. They will keep your mind free to respond appropriately and problem-solve effectively when you are under the stress of trying a case, negotiating a settlement, or taking a deposition.

These abilities are a big part of what makes a lawyer successful. Thus, if you can master them on the bar exam, chances are you can master them in the practice of law as well.

Good luck.

# BIBLIOGRAPHY

Davies, Don. "Maximizing Examination Performance: A Psychological Approach." New York and London: Nichols Publishing Company. 1986

Johnson, Susan. "Taking the Anxiety Out of Taking Tests: A Step-by-Step Guide." Berkeley: New Harbinger Publications, Inc., 1997

Philips, Robert H. "Reduce Your Test Anxiety: 128 Strategies to Help You Make the Grade." New York: Balance Enterprises, Inc., 1996

Purkey, William Watson. "What Students Say To Themselves: Internal Dialogue and School Success." California: Corwin Press, Inc., 2000

Sapp, Marty. "Test Anxiety: Applied Research, Assessment, and Treatment Interventions," 2nd ed., Maryland and Oxford: University Press of America, Inc., 1999

Scruggs, Thomas E. and Margo A. Mastropieri. "Teaching Test-Taking Skills: Helping Students Show What They Know." Purdue University: Brookline Books, 1992

Zeidner, Moshe. "Test Anxiety: The State of the Art." New York and London: Plenum Press, 1998